The
Journey
of the
Black Heart

Blake Blackman

Highway 51 Publishing, LLC
Mint Hill, North Carolina
HWY51.com

Published by Highway 51 Publishing, LLC
Mint Hill, North Carolina
HWY51.com

ISBN: 0996057021
ISBN-13: 978-0-9960570-2-8

Library of Congress Control Number: 2015947758

All scripture quotations are taken from the Holy Bible, New International Version®, NIV®. Copyright ©1973, 1978, 1984, 2011 by Biblica, Inc.™ Used by permission of Zondervan. All rights reserved worldwide. www.zondervan.com The "NIV" and "New International Version" are trademarks registered in the United States Patent and Trademark Office by Biblica, Inc.™

Page 111
THIS MUST BE THE PLACE (NAIVE MELODY)
Words and Music by DAVID BYRNE CHRIS FRANTZ, JERRY
HARRISON and TINA WEYMOUTH
© 1983 WB MUSIC CORP. and INDEX MUSIC, INC.
All rights administered by WB MUSIC CORP.
All Rights Reserved

Page 141
Language Or The Kiss
Words and Music by Emily Saliers
Copyright (c) 1994 GODHAP MUSIC
All Rights Administered by SONGS OF UNIVERSAL, INC.
All Rights Reserved Used by Permission
Reprinted by Permission of Hal Leonard Corporation

Although the stories told in this book are true, some names have been changed or omitted to protect the privacy of individuals.

Front and back cover design: Steven Mast, Glyph Design Group, glyphdesigngroup.com
Author photo: ©2015 Sarah DeShields,
Editing: Kristen Driscoll, Highway 51 Publishing

For my Noah.

You are my story worth telling.

Dear Jon,

I'm so thankful you're pastoring
Renovatus AND that I get to be a part
of what the Lord is doing there now!
I'm really looking forward to what
all is coming!

Blake

CONTENTS

FOREWORD

I don't know how to prepare you for what you will experience in the pages ahead, because I'm not entirely sure how to prepare you for Blake. The book, like her, kind of just *has to happen to you.*

I'm struck by just how it embodies everything that she is—at high voltage. I'm not sure how you get this much tenderness and toughness into one book, or how you wrap together this much hope and heartbreak. I don't know how *The Journey of the Black Heart* manages to be alternately as artful, earthy, funny, wise, or textured as it is. I only know that it's a book brimming with the ache that makes us human. It is all the things life is, simultaneously. It is lightning in a bottle. In other words, it is very much like Blake herself.

I came to know her about midway through the story she tells here, when she worked the front of The Common Market deli and I was an upstart young pastor. The kindness of heart was so apparent even then; the purity of spirit and conviction; the earthy, profane eloquence and unforced poetry of her stories. But those were days when she wore a lot of hurt on her sleeve, too, the hurts she writes about so eloquently here. We liked each other instantly, which made way for the friendship she describes later in the book. I wouldn't want to oversimplify any of it, but I think it's pretty fair to say that we had a tacit agreement: She taught me about the world, and I taught her about Jesus, which worked out really well for both of us. It wasn't too long after that Blake was playing a central role in the church we had started, and we were dreaming and scheming on how to love our city together.

We've been friends long enough now for our roles to have since reversed. When I felt like my world was crashing down, Blake was the one teaching me about Jesus—sometimes through her own stories, sometimes repeating my own words back to me. She was reminding me of all the ways God had met her in her own shame and guilt and loss, like she does here. She was the one telling me that I could and would survive. Blake's famous for being a big talker, but the truths of her stories are even bigger, so I believed her. They carried me, as I trust they will carry you.

I remember distinctly, in the moments when the fog was the thickest and the night the longest, just how much I just loved to hear Blake pray. Sometimes even something simple, like the way she'd pray before a meal, was so earnest and authentic, so heavenly and yet so tethered to the ground, that it would bring my own feet back down to earth, even if just for a minute.

I've now taken solace in Blake's stories of life and loss and Jesus more times than I can remember. I would feel stingy to keep them to myself, even though Blake's the rare friend you get in your life you would just as soon not share with anyone else. But she's also the best storyteller I know, and I've known since I met her that her stories had the weight of destiny on them. I've always been eager for the day that, rather than keeping them at home, she would put them on the bus—like kids bundled up for the first day of school—and release them into the world. The fact that you're reading these stories now means they have arrived at the city of their final destination.

Last year, Blake introduced me to Patti Smith's haunting memoir, *Just Kids*, and it instantly became one of my favorite

FOREWORD

books. In the book, she asks, "Why can't I write something that would awake the dead? That pursuit is what burns most deeply." I think the highest compliment I could pay Blake here is that she has written a book that would make Patti proud. This is a book that awakens the dead.

Jonathan Martin

INTRODUCTION

I don't have a vocabulary full of ten-dollar words. I never came close to finishing college. Because of that, my entire adult life I have struggled with the feeling that I am not very smart. The idea that I would write a book has always seemed absurd to me.

I was close to thirty years old before I began to have a real relationship with Jesus, and from early on in that experience I have felt like the Lord has impressed deep into my soul his desire for me to write. There have been some fits and starts here and there because I could never escape the nagging feeling that that's what I'm supposed to be doing, but, ultimately, because of my fear of being seen as not very smart, I've always laid it back down.

Recently, I left my job at the church where I fell in love with Jesus. I've had no idea where to go or what to do next. This season in my life has been a brutal one, one that has left me questioning my identity, beliefs, and, ultimately, what to do with this messy life of mine. I remember reading Barbara Brown Taylor in *An Altar in the World*. She tells how she graduated from college and so desperately wanted to do whatever the Lord wanted with her life. She would pray and pray, asking God to tell her what he wanted from her. When the answer finally came, he simply said, "Love me and do what you like." I remember laying in bed one night mulling this over and being absolutely horrified. That's fine for Barbara; she went on to be a priest and a professor. At this juncture in my life, I am thirty-seven years old, with no education and few marketable skills, other than being the most talkative people person you ever knew. But I don't think anyone is going to pay me for that.

I told the Lord that I would do literally anything he asked of me, but that because he knows all of his children, even every hair on our heads, I desperately needed him to tell me what he would have me do. How would my life best serve him? How can I join him in doing what I can to push back the darkness a little each day? I was fully prepared for him to answer me with, "Take care of your family," or "Go back to school." Those answers would have satisfied me.

But as I was lying in bed one night, wrestling with the Lord for a blessing, once again all he said was "Write."

So I am, and I will.

The Gospels say that everyone knew the disciples were not educated men, but when they heard them speak, they knew they had been with Jesus. That is all my heart hopes for in these pages. I will write these words he has asked me to write, and I will hold them in my open palm for him to do with what he will. But I will pray, pray, pray as I go that after you read them you will know I have been with Jesus.

~

As long as I have been an adult woman—and I use that term loosely because I had my first son at twenty-one and that made me feel pretty adult, even though I was still just a kid—I have understood that childbirth and mothering are huge, life-altering events for women. I don't mean that in the "middle of the night feedings, I now have no social life, and my body looks different," kind of way. I mean something about the very knitting together of the insides of these women has changed. This was never more evident than when

INTRODUCTION

I became a Christian. By the time I began attending
Renovatus Church, my son Noah was already eight years old
and I was twenty-nine. The church consisted mostly of young
couples who had not yet begun to grow their families. I was a
single mom without much religious background, swimming in
a sea of childless married couples who had adored Jesus most
of their lives.

Then, there are the books I've read over the years, books
by strong, beautiful, Christian women. A Christian woman
almost can't write a book without going into great detail
about the birth of her babies, making a connection between
their births and the birth of Jesus (I don't mean that to sound
like a jab), and then telling all of the ways her relationship
with her child(ren) has revealed the heart of God to her.
These stories are gorgeous and even inviting in some ways. I
leave these stories wanting so badly to have had the same
experiences or, at the very least, to understand theirs. But I
don't.

Motherhood didn't happen like that for me, and, try as I
might with my now sixteen-year-old, I just can't seem to
muster those kinds of memories or experiences. They simply
aren't there. I read those books, hear those stories, and want
to scream: "What about the women like me? Who will tell our
stories? Surely, I am not alone!" Several months ago, I was
out to dinner with a friend of mine. She was talking about
launching a blog and writing all the things she thinks and feels
and the things the Lord puts on her heart. She had the exact
fears I do—that she doesn't have anything original to say or
that we haven't all heard before. Then she said God reminded
her that there really are no new stories under the sun. Even
the Bible is a collection of repeats—stories of heartbreak,
grief, joy, repentance, gratitude, salvation, peace, fear,
redemption, and such. The best and sweetest gift we can give
to the world is to share our part of the story. It's how we
survive and keep going to face another day, by the strength
we gain from one another.

So, I'm doing it. I'm going to allow my story to join the

multitudes of other witnesses who have gone before me and who are moving alongside me right now. Mine is a story wrought with grief but also redemption. Many of us didn't live our lives in order. Mine has been *decidedly* out of order. But God makes sense of chaos. For all of us whose lives seem to have an "Out of Order" sign hung on our necks, there's a place for us.

CHAPTER ONE
THE END

Where was God? I knew exactly where God was. He was off somewhere in the cosmos killing my baby, and I hated him for it. And there I was, only three or four months after he died, sitting in a little office with Dawn, a woman only a couple of years older than I, talking through the details of that past year or so. She was a Buddhist and I was a nothing, so I thought this could work out. I certainly didn't want some Jesus freak breathing down my neck, trying to get me to pinpoint where I felt God was in all this.

I have been in and out of counseling for years, most notably, this stretch after my son Zyler died in 2001. For twenty years, my mother worked at the preschool at the Jewish Community Center in Charlotte. "The J," as we familiarly called it, had a counseling department for members. After Zyler's death, my mom was determined to get me in to see someone. To say I didn't want to go is an understatement.

So, what the hell was I supposed to say? I told Dawn all the events in quite a matter of fact way. I didn't cry. I didn't lose it. I just told her everything that had happened, and I didn't understand why we couldn't just be done, then. For good. After a few sessions over the course of a few weeks, I had no idea why I was supposed to continue to see this woman. What were we supposed to talk about? She knew the events. I had told someone the situation. Surely, that was enough to get my mom off my back?

One day, Dawn asked if I thought I was fully experiencing and feeling my grief. I didn't know! I asked her what that meant. How was grief supposed to go? Is there a workbook, a guide, an instruction manual? I would've been happy to "work the steps" like an alcoholic in an AA program, if at the end I could say I worked through my grief and arrived on the other side. Then I could move on with my life, putting this irritating grief business behind me.

I don't mean to sound callous, really, I don't. But my husband, Zach, had gone back to work just two days after Zyler's funeral, and I had three-year-old Noah at home to care for. What I would have given to have been Jewish during those first few weeks. At least in their tradition they have the gift of sitting Shiva for seven days following the death. They cover the mirrors in their homes, sit on low chairs, and people stop by to pay their condolences. It seems they take the time to actually feel the weight of their missing family member and do their best to prepare for a life lived without them. But for me, not one person came to my rescue or even brought me a meal. Not one. No one offered to keep my remaining son, Noah, so I could lie in bed and cry all day. So I figured if the world had moved on, I might as well, too. Experience my grief? What the hell did that even mean?

Zyler was born with two holes in his heart and needed to have them repaired before he went into kindergarten. His father and I set the surgery date for December 4, 2001, only two weeks after his first birthday. We absolutely didn't want him to have any memory of the surgery.

He was always a happy baby. That's not just fluffy nostalgia. He really was always happy. He only cried when he was hungry. So, when we arrived at the hospital at 5:30 a.m. for surgery prep, he was happy then, too. After he was checked in, we just waited and waited. Surgery wasn't until 7:30, and clearly it doesn't take two hours to prep someone.

I've had several surgeries myself through the years, and I've always wondered why you have to show up so early. I think it's so you can sit there long enough to get good and scared over what's about to happen to you.

It turns out that fear is just as potent when you're waiting for someone else—namely, your one-year-old son—to have heart surgery. He was just so little. How do you open the chest of a baby and operate on his heart? Isn't it just *too little*?

Zyler wasn't quite walking on his own yet that morning. He was a bit of a late bloomer in that department. So, before they put him to sleep, they brought in this big, plastic, toy wagon. Zyler grabbed the handle of that wagon and pushed it around and around our little prep area, giggling the whole time. I was so thankful he was having fun and also feeling so guilty because he had no idea of the ordeal ahead.

Eventually, a nurse came in and gave him medication by mouth to make him drowsy. Sweet, little Zyler giggled and cooed his way to sleep in my arms, and that was the last time I ever held him alive.

My mom and dad came to wait with us, and one of my closest friends, who lived two hours away, was there bright and early at 7:30. Zach and I sat with them in the waiting room, barely daring to breathe or speak for hours. The surgery was supposed to have taken a solid five hours. But after only three or four hours, the doctor came out and let us know that all had gone fine, better than expected, actually.

The relief I felt—I don't think I have ever felt a weight lift from me like I did in that moment. I had gone into the hospital that morning half-convinced that something terrible was going to happen during Zyler's surgery. So when the doctor said he was doing great and we could go get lunch and see him afterward, well, there are no words for the happiness and freedom I felt.

The rest of that Monday was relatively uneventful. We ate, Mom and Dad left feeling so very happy and grateful, and my husband and I were allowed to go in and visit our son in the heart recovery unit. We were only allowed in every two hours for fifteen minutes at a time, but that was enough. He was so small and asleep and working to heal from his big surgery. But he was alive, and he would heal, and we could all go home and create a good normal, maybe for the first time in his short life.

My husband and I planned to spend the night at least that first night and maybe every other night, too, but definitely the first night. Zyler had to stay in the heart recovery unit with several different patients. Then, the next day, if all progressed smoothly, he would be moved into a private room.

We went up for our 8 p.m. visit and rang the little doorbell. The sweet, elderly, volunteer lady came to the door. She told us that they had a patient coming up from surgery so they couldn't let us in right now. Give them a few minutes to get him settled, and then we could come in. I was feeling so happy. We each went to the restroom, and when we came out, we met in the hall and laughed and kissed. We were just so thankful for Zyler's life and that the anticipation of the surgery was over, the surgery itself was over, and all was well. I distinctly remember that moment in the hallway and the gratitude that was in it.

When the huge, double doors to the heart recovery unit were open, you could see straight across the room to Zyler's bed. His was the first one, and they all went in a semi-circle from there. When we returned from using the restroom, none of the other families who had been there previously waiting to visit their loved ones were in the hall. We assumed that was because they had already been allowed inside. So, we rang the doorbell once again, and the volunteer came to the door again. But this time we could see Zyler's bed and the panic in this lady's eyes. The curtain was drawn around his bed, and we could see probably six or eight sets of feet under that curtain.

The lady said, "We've been looking for you. There's a problem with the baby." Of everything that ended up happening the next few days, I believe those were the most devastating words I heard throughout the whole experience. In the depths of my gut, I knew. I knew it didn't work, and I knew he wasn't going to be OK, and I knew he wasn't coming home. I could feel those things like someone had come along and written them on my insides. And then I wondered if that patient ever did come up from surgery?

We were escorted to a tiny—and I mean tiny—room around the corner. The volunteer lady asked us to wait in there until the doctor could come and speak with us. We waited and waited, frustrated that there wasn't enough room to pace the floor. So, we sat. We sat up on the couch, we leaned back on the couch, and we moved from the couch to the chair. But we didn't cry. Neither of us cried. We did, however, hold each other's hands, look each other in the eye and say, "OK, he's dead. This is taking too long. They couldn't save him, and they don't know how to tell us. What do we do first? Do we go tell my mother? We can't deliver news like this on the phone."

Even now, all these years later, the memory of my husband and I in that microscopic room makes me so sad. No parents should have to have that conversation. It's like we were doing our best to psych ourselves up for the fact he was dead. We needed to be prepared. No surprises.

We did end up being surprised, one surprise right after another. First, hospital clergy showed up. Nowadays, I think the idea of hospital clergy is lovely. But back then, I wasn't interested in God, and I absolutely wasn't interested in a stranger sitting in the room with me while I waited for the worst news of my life. And not just any stranger, but one who I figured was there to proselytize and tell me that God has a purpose in everything.

As soon as she walked into the room and told me who she was, I was pretty sure this experience was going to conclude with me punching her in the nose. I was sure she was going to ask if she could pray with us, and I was going to be able to take out all my fear and anger on her when she did. The fact that I didn't get a chance to punch her did make it awfully awkward for her to be in that tiny-ass room. We all just sat silently waiting on the doctor to come in. I wasn't about to talk with my husband about my real feelings and fears in front of her.

After forty-five minutes, the doctor came in. I don't even remember that man's name because he wasn't Zyler's primary doc, but his assistant. How about that? My son is crashing and dying, and we have the assistant. When he walked into the room, the front of his scrubs were covered in blood. Zyler's blood. I didn't realize a one-year-old could have that much blood inside his or her little body. He didn't bother to put on one of those white overcoats things they wear or anything. He was visibly panicked and talking so fast we could barely keep up.

The gist of it was that Zyler had gone into cardiac arrest, and they had no idea why. They had his chest opened and had been manually pumping his heart with their hands for forty-five minutes. Up until this point, his heart had not begun to beat again on its own. They were also manually administering oxygen by pumping a bag over his mouth and nose. They were going to continue to try to get his heart to come back on its own. Then the assistant left the room. That was it. And again I thought, *How do you open a baby's chest and pump his heart with your hands? Isn't he just too little?*

Basically, my baby had died. They decided to try to revive him and it wasn't working, but they were going to keep trying. That's when it began, right there in the moment that doctor walked out of our tiny hell. My husband, Zach, began to hope and believe against all hope and belief. He believed that Zyler's heart would come back on its own and that he would make a complete recovery. Zach let himself imagine a future for our family where we were all healthy and happy and together. Beginning right then, he found the strength to survive the heartbreak we were about to embark on.

I did not. In that same moment, I knew our son would never be whole again. I knew he had gone too long without proper oxygen to his brain. I fully understood that he had been dead for close to an hour, and he wasn't going to just recover. I knew it was over.

Another forty-five minutes passed, and the doc came back in. Zyler's heart never did begin to beat on its own, so they had set him up on a life-support machine called an ECMO. This machine would pump his heart for him and provide some respiratory support, as well.

I was crushed that they chose to put him on life support. At this point, he had been dead for an hour and a half. You don't come back from that. You just don't. But Zach was so hopeful. He was convinced they wouldn't have put him on the life support if they didn't think there was a chance. I was much more skeptical and was sure they put him on that machine to cover their own asses. I wasn't sure what they had done wrong, but I was sure they had done something.

At eleven o' clock that night, worn out and bruised from the day, Zach and I made the forty-minute drive to my parent's house. This wasn't the kind of news you deliver on the phone if you don't have to. My mom was still up watching TV, and she says that when she heard our car doors shut in the driveway, she knew and her stomach leapt into her throat. She woke Dad up, and we told them everything. We all sat in the living room and smoked cigarettes, no one talking, everyone in shock and dry-eyed except for my sweet, sweet father who sat and silently cried while he smoked.

Thus began the hardest eleven days of my life. Zach and I lived at the hospital. They were very kind and gave us a giant, private waiting room to ourselves. It had two couches and plenty of chairs, a TV, and a bathroom. The hospital gave us parking passes and meal comps for the cafeteria and even brought by a snack basket every single day. At the time, I thought they were so sweet and kind. They clearly felt really sorry for us and all we were going through. The more I look back, though, the more I wonder. Was all that just another way they were trying to pacify us so we didn't sue the shit out of them? I'll never know.

Zyler never woke up. He never moved into his own

room. He stayed in the heart recovery unit the entire eleven days. All in all, they had to open his chest three times after his surgery to pump his heart or adjust the ECMO machine. He had a team of thirteen doctors, heart surgeons, kidney specialists, neurologists, etc. There was always someone checking him, poking him, running tests on him. They abandoned the every two hours rule for my husband and I. We could come and go as often as we liked because everyone knew Zyler was dying. Everyone, but Zach.

Zach and I had never had much relationship with God or the church. But during Zyler's short life we had visited a church a few times with some friends. Zach seemed to enjoy church, but once Zyler's surgery went all wrong, he suddenly had faith that would move mountains. With every negative test result, my poor sweet husband believed more firmly. I have no idea the number of prayers he offered up during those days, but, surely, they number in the thousands.

I don't think I prayed much at all. I had no hope. With every EEG, the news of Zyler's brain was bleaker than the one before. By day seven or eight, the EEG revealed that he was blind. If you opened his eyes and looked in, they were clouded over, and that would never be corrected. Eventually, his kidneys began to shut down and he developed pneumonia. Ironically, his heart did slowly begin to beat on its own again, but it was too late. The rest of his body was shutting down.

I had no hope, and still, somehow, Zach never lost his.

On December 14, 2001, literally the five-year anniversary of my first date with Zach, we had a meeting with Zyler's medical team. The night before, Zach and I went home and slept in our own bed. I stayed up after him and watched *Steel Magnolias*. I had barely cried in the last ten days, and I needed to let it out. I had seen that movie a hundred times, but watching M'Lynn decide to turn off her daughter's life support took on a whole new meaning that night. It's a terrible thing having your child die before you, but it is a whole other hell to know it's coming and to know it will be you that says, "Turn it off." That is hell.

Believe it or not, we did sleep. Zach woke up bright and early, wanting to get to the hospital to spend as much time with Zyler as possible before noon. I stayed behind at the house wanting to be alone for a while. I showered and even put on a little makeup. I stood in my closet for the longest time trying to decide what to wear. I needed to choose something that I didn't like very much because I would never want to wear it again. After today, it would always be the shirt I was wearing when my baby died. I picked an ugly sweater and left.

My whole family came. They crowded into that private waiting room that had felt so big when it was only Zach and I but felt unbearably small that morning. Zach would scarcely leave Zyler's bedside; I would scarcely go in. Looking back, I can see the walls I began putting up the very day of his surgery. I gave myself rough edges from the start, so hoping that none of this hurt could make its way into my heart. I tried so very hard not to feel one damn bit of any of it.

Zach and I said goodbye together. My mom went and said her goodbye. And then the family waited while we met with the medical team. It was an oval table with roughly ten to twelve doctors sitting around it. It felt so intimidating, a room full of doctors and there was Zach and me, just a couple of twenty-four- and twenty-five-year-old kids, too young to be making decisions like this.

Thankfully, Dr. Holt, our pediatrician, was there; she was always there. The entire eleven days, she just kept showing up when we least expected her but desperately needed her. She had been a friend of my mom and aunt for years, and every time she walked in the room, it felt like family. She was such a comfort and support. She never minced words and always let us know how bad it truly was. That may sound harsh, but I needed the truth. I couldn't have handled being blindsided by what was about to be said to me in this meeting.

We sat across from the heart doctors and next to the neurologist, strangely enough named Dr. Hart. She did all the talking, all of it. She explained that they had run three EEGs in the course of the last eleven days, each one progressively worse than the last. In short, Zyler was brain dead, and that was never going to change. I knew what was coming next before she said it.

She explained our options:

Zyler's heart would eventually be able to function completely on it's own. *Isn't that just cruel?* I thought. *The thing we brought him into the hospital for would one day be well and whole. But somehow you jerks managed to make my baby brain dead in the fixing of his heart.* So we could leave Zyler hooked up to life support forever, and he very well could live into his twenties. Of course, he would never wake up. Ever. Or have any quality of life. None. And neither would we because he could never be left alone, and we would have tremendous medical expenses and equipment all through our house. Noah would never have a normal childhood because our immediate priority would be Zyler's care, but, hey, we could keep him alive into his twenties if that was our choice.

Or, the other option was that we could choose to turn off the machines today and let him go. Zach and I had already made the decision but sitting there hearing Dr. Hart say it out loud made it so real and final. It was time. It wasn't like yesterday or the day before when he and I were sitting in the cafeteria talking through our options. It was now, and very soon our son would be gone. It was now.

As long as I live, I will always remember the next moment. Zach and I sat there panicked and overwhelmed. We had made a choice, but we didn't know how to say it. I think I finally began to cry a little, and we just sat there not wanting to say the words. Then, as if we shared a brain, we both looked down the long table to where Dr. Holt sat, with our eyes begging for an answer. With her eyes filled with tears, she simply nodded her head *yes*, and I couldn't have been more grateful for that tiniest grace. Our pediatrician gave me one of the greatest gifts a human being could have given me in that moment: permission.

Zach and I turned to Dr. Hart and said, "Let's turn off the machines."

Noah hadn't seen his little brother since we admitted him to the hospital, and we figured it would be best for him to have a chance to say goodbye. I was sure it would mess him up six ways to Sunday for his brother to just disappear out of his life. Our sweet nurses unplugged Zyler from all the big, scary machines that might traumatize Noah forever. Zyler didn't need those things now, anyway. They kept him attached to his morphine, but that was all.

We went and got Noah, and the three of us sat on Zyler's bedside and told him goodbye. Noah kissed his little face, told him he loved him, that he would miss him, and he was a good brother. He asked to see Zyler's chest, and we kept having to tell him no. He said he wanted to see his broken heart. Tears ran down my cheeks as I thought of all Noah was losing that day and realized that for the rest of my life no one would be able to see my broken heart.

After we took Noah back downstairs, it was time. A bunch of my family huddled together in a little private room near Zyler's bed. I can't remember which family members came. I know my Mom stayed downstairs with Noah. She said she couldn't see this next part. I sat in a rocking chair, and they placed my baby in my arms for the last time.

Zach sat next to me, and we took turns holding him as we watched the screen monitoring his heartbeat beep slower and slower. I was holding him when it finally stopped. The nurse removed the monitor from his hand and, one-by-one, my family left. Zach and I just sat holding his lifeless body and caressing his head.

How long do you sit and hold your dead baby? *Once they take him, I'll never see him again*, I thought. *I better make this count, me and my ugly sweater.* I actually don't think we held him all that long. I watched the nurse as he took Zyler back to his bed and laid him there to wait for the funeral home to come and get him.

We went downstairs to see my family. They were mostly

silent when we came into the room. What were they supposed to say? And, again, one by one, they all left. Mom took Noah with her. She just wanted to be near Noah, and I was thankful because I certainly didn't know how to be a parent that day.

Zach and I had come in separate cars, and that was a grace, too. We had no idea how to comfort each other, so he decided to go to a movie alone. That's what Zach did when he couldn't process a thing; he went to the movies. I know a lot of people find that strange, but I have never been upset or hurt by his choice. It seems perfectly logical to me that a person would want to hide and pretend that this reality was not their reality for one afternoon. There is no way of knowing what you are supposed to do or feel.

Eventually, I was alone in that big waiting room, and that was just fine with me. The words "Dead baby, you have a dead baby," rang over and over in my ears. More than once I considered running back upstairs and grabbing Zyler and taking him home. I wanted to lie in bed and hold him, just the two of us, willing him to live. I was certain it would work. Oddly, now that he was actually gone, I thought I could pray him back to life. Finally, I found my prayers. I thought of Lazarus and Jesus' miracles, and I thought maybe, just maybe, God had one in store for me.

But instead I just sat, numb and in disbelief, until someone from the hospital came in with a beautiful little box for me. Inside the box was a lock of Zyler's hair, his hospital bracelet, and Polaroid pictures of Zach and I holding him after he had already died. I didn't remember anyone taking our picture but, apparently, they did. I definitely couldn't ever wear that damn sweater again.

I left the hospital alone and went to a favorite diner to get take out. I had a Jack and Coke while I waited for it. Sitting at the bar, some guy who had had too many drinks at three in the afternoon actually tried to hit on me. Today, I still think that was one of the funniest experiences of my life.

He sidled up next to me and asked, "Rough day? Why

don't you let me buy you a drink and you can tell me all about it?"

I chose to be polite, "Thanks, but no, thanks." I wanted to stand on that bar and shout to the entire room that my baby died today and what the hell were they all doing eating burgers, drinking beer, and laughing like the whole world didn't just come to an end? In the end, I went home alone and stared at the food instead of eating it.

It's been a little over twelve years since Zyler died. I know memories become foggy as time marches on, but the things I saw during those eleven days—and the hurts and betrayal I felt—will forever be etched like a laser to my soul. I can see the hospital, the waiting room, his broken body. That's the worst part. We can't un-see the things we've seen. They're always there. They always haunt you. Forever.

CHAPTER TWO
FUCK THIS TIME AND PLACE

I have no idea why I made some of the choices I made when I was younger. Sure, parts of my childhood were hard, damn hard, but that's true for everyone. My mom and I didn't get along until I was well into my twenties, we were dirt poor, and sometimes my daddy had a drinking problem. Even still, when I look back, I have never been able to pinpoint precisely what made me choose the things I did. Deep down, I knew I was blowing up my life. Somewhere inside, I knew I was making choices that I wouldn't be able to recover from. Still, I have always been ridiculously stubborn, and I think I wanted to prove that I was the exception not the rule. It turns out I wasn't.

I attended a small, all-girls, Christian college in Raleigh. Almost twenty years later, I laugh right out loud when I read that sentence. I thought it was a good idea for this girl whose personality tests always indicate a need to be *against* to attend an all-girl Christian college. I knew myself better than that.

I was supposed to attend Appalachian State in Boone. I had already spoken with my roommate and started to make plans for our first year together. But over the summer, at the last minute, I chickened out. I couldn't live that far away from Rosa, my best friend since age five, who was going to Chapel

Hill. I guess I wasn't quite as independent as I thought. So, I switched to Meredith where I would be only thirty minutes from her. That felt much safer.

I didn't last a full year in that place. I wasn't really a Christian, and I have always been just about as anti-establishment as I could be without doing something crazy, like completely going off the grid. Plus, like a lot of young women in college, I went through the whole "Am I a lesbian?" phase. I wasn't, but it wasn't for lack of exploration. There was a girl, and not only did I think I loved her, but she was trouble in general, and I went along every time. I never found myself *in* the trouble but was always getting her out of hers. By the spring semester, I was confused, afraid, homesick for the mother I didn't get along with, and experiencing anxiety attacks. Log this as mistake number one.

Mistake number two was dropping out of that college. I was so pitiful and scared that Mom and Dad let me drop out of my freshman year on April 1, my birthday. I came home with my tail tucked between my legs, leaving behind trouble girl and my dream of being the first in my family to go to college. Well, technically I guess you could say I went. I just didn't finish.

I grew up in the town of Monroe just about forty minutes east of Charlotte. Monroe isn't all that big, and the two little, tiny towns as you continue east, Wingate and Marshville, are even smaller. My high school was in Marshville, home of Randy Travis, and everyone was black or white, no variation of brown whatsoever. If anyone down there was gay, we certainly didn't know it, and you naturally assumed everyone was a Christian. There were absolutely no Jews or Buddhists. I don't even think we knew what the word *Atheist* meant.

When my mother began to travel to Charlotte to work at the Jewish Community Center, imagine me trying to explain to my friends and their parents what my mom did for a living. In Union County, if you didn't teach or farm turkeys, then you may as well have been from another country.

Looking back, I think I was so convinced of the ignorance and small-mindedness of the people where I grew up that I was desperate to get out of there. I wanted to go somewhere more progressive, like the Research Triangle, Raleigh. I wanted to find my people, the liberals. I suppose in some ways that was mistake number three. I'm still a liberal and still pretty anti-establishment but not nearly so cocky and self-righteous. Those folks where I grew up are good folks. We're just different.

Not long after I dropped out of school, I moved to Charlotte with a couple of girls I had gone to high school with. We moved in time for the next school year to start because they were going to UNCC. I wasn't.

I was learning what it meant to be a working girl. I have no idea how I actually paid my bills. My parents didn't have two pennies to rub together, so no money came from them, and the jobs I had during that year had to have all been paying little over minimum wage. But somehow I paid my share and still had money for food and gas.

In December it happened—the thing that changed everything. I met the boy.

I always liked boys. I mean I really liked boys, and there was never a shortage of them. I grew up five minutes from Wingate University and worked at the only grocery store in town. There was no lack of boys! In school, two boys were my best-est friends for years. I almost always had a boyfriend. I had relationships with two different boys that were taboo, and we had to keep them somewhat under the radar. Yet, none of those boys even came close to "the boy."

We met so innocently. I was helping a friend move from a dorm room to an apartment. The apartment had four bedrooms, and one guy had just moved out, and my friend had answered the ad for a room for rent. In late November or early December, I went with him to his new place and started helping him unload boxes. When we walked in the door the first time, one of my friend's new roommates came out of his bedroom and offered to help us. Game over. I had no way of knowing this was the moment that would change my life forever.

His name was Zach, and he was unlike any guy I had ever met before. The word *confident* just doesn't do him justice. He had long hair and owned two cars, a Jetta and a Wrangler. He had only one arm because of an accident when he was fifteen. He hadn't gone to college but worked at a local bakery/café chain, instead. He could fix just about anything on those two cars, even with only one arm. He had no real family ties, with his father living in Virginia and his mom and sister in California. He was a loner with few friends, so at twenty that made him mysterious and alluring to me.

He smoked American Spirit cigarettes when I smoked Camels. I had never heard of his brand so automatically that made him cooler, too. And he introduced me to Cat Stevens and Van Morrison, so that made him deep.

I was done in. I could do nothing except go along for the ride.

Not long after we began dating that December, Zach told me of his plan to move to California the following June. He had grown up without his mom and sister and had decided it was time to do life with them for a while. Even though we had only been seeing each other for a minute, we were too smitten to be separated from one another. There was no way he was moving to the other side of the country without me! And there we have mistake number four.

By early June, we had quit our jobs, sold or thrown away everything that wouldn't fit into his Jetta, and helped our roommates find someone to rent our rooms. The night before we set out for the Great West Coast, my family had a little going away dinner at an Italian restaurant. My aunts and siblings were there and my parents. Zach and I were so excited and happy that night that I thought we would pee our pants. My parents looked as if someone had ripped their hearts out, and they would barely even glance in Zach's direction. Whether they had liked him before was irrelevant.

The fact that he was taking their twenty-year-old daughter 3,000 miles away made him the world's biggest son of a bitch.

The next morning, we set off driving across this massive country of ours, Berkeley-bound; listening to Ani Difranco and smoking clove cigarettes. At night, we drove into the most beautiful lightning storm in Kansas and found a head shop in downtown St. Louis to buy cloves. We ate buffalo burgers in Jackson Hole, and on the bank of the Snake River we promised to love each other, forever. And then, around five one afternoon, we crossed into California, giddy and full of expectation about what our future in this foreign land would bring. Around eight, we pulled into his mom's driveway, worn out and content. I couldn't wait to meet her and Zach's twelve-year-old half-brother. She also had a male roommate, who she claimed was not her boyfriend. They were just friends who lived together because it was more affordable than living alone.

As I stood in the apartment complex parking lot my first night in Berkeley, I had no idea what all I was in for the next few months. All in all, I stayed there less than six months, but, somehow, it managed to feel like a lifetime.

People in Berkeley are different, much different than the people of the South. Their culture is different; their lifestyle is different. Everything is different. It would be absolutely fair to say I had a hard time adjusting.

Zach's mom lived in a two-bedroom apartment, and now I lived in that same two-bedroom apartment with her. She and the roommate had decided to sleep together on the foldout couch so Zach and I could have the second bedroom. The half-brother had the first. To prepare for our arrival, Mom had taken all of the things she had been keeping in that room and packed them in boxes from the liquor store. Then, she stacked those boxes floor to ceiling in that second bedroom. I remember wondering just what the hell she could possibly have in all those boxes, but I was too afraid to ask. She may just spend an entire day showing me. Of course, I was interested in Zach's baby pictures or elementary school awards, but I wasn't willing to go through the rest of this woman's life to get to them.

Where were we supposed to put our stuff? Granted, we hadn't brought much, but we needed somewhere to put it. I don't remember a dresser or even closet space. I think we lived out of our suitcases, which sat on the floor in the corner of the room.

I was already on the verge of hyperventilating about the lack of space in the room, and then I saw it. Mom pointed it out. She was so proud of herself. This was clearly a woman who did not operate at 100 percent, but I didn't know that. I don't think Zach knew before that first night. They hadn't seen each other often while he was growing up, so he didn't know that his mother was the type of woman who would find a used, tossed out, futon mattress on the side of the road and jump for joy at her good fortune. He didn't know she was the type of woman who would bring that mattress home, drag it up two flights of stairs, and place it in on the floor in the middle of a room full of liquor store boxes for her son and his girlfriend to sleep on, even though it was covered in blood. Yes, blood!

Mom didn't bother to put sheets on the mattress before we got there. She showed us to our room and showed that mattress off as if it were her proudest accomplishment. She never acknowledged the blood. I don't know if she was hoping we wouldn't notice, or if she had not noticed herself. I have a feeling she's the type of lady who wouldn't care what was on a mattress as long as it was free.

Zach and I smiled politely and thanked her for getting it for us. We asked for sheets, and she provided some. That first night, we didn't stay up late catching up. We unloaded what we needed from the car, put the sheets on the bed, and went to sleep with our dreams of California a little more sober and realistic than they had been only a few hours earlier.

We both got jobs, but neither of them paid much, and California is expensive. I didn't know how we would ever move out of his mother's house, and I desperately needed to move out. She and his half-brother and the roommate were all just entirely too strange for me. We didn't speak the same language, and I didn't know how to learn theirs.

The roommate was probably around sixty but I thought he looked closer to eighty. Neither of them worked, collecting disability instead, which made sense for the roommate because he didn't seem to be able to walk very well. But I couldn't understand what Mom's disability was. I mean, sure, she didn't seem to be all there mentally, but I still thought there could've been some kind of job for her. The half-brother barely spoke or interacted in any way. He stayed in his room, watching TV or playing video games. He went to school but that was the extent of that. He showed up, giving no further thought or effort, otherwise.

I finally met Zach's sister a couple of weeks after we arrived. She was a year-and-a-half older than him and had a two-year-old daughter. Zach loved her so much and spoke highly of her, so I was quite excited to meet her. I was lonesome and homesick and hoped I would find a friend in her. Maybe she would introduce us to her friends, and we would start to have a little social life, because up to that point, we just worked and spent time together. We had realized that happy, little family dinners weren't going to be our new normal with his mom, so sometimes we would just stay out until it was time to go to bed. One could say a lot of hope rested on this sister.

Sister was a hippie in ways I had only seen in movies. She didn't shave her legs or arm pits, and I'm pretty sure she didn't eat meat. She did eat things I had never heard of, like pesto and arugula, and it didn't seem as if daily bathing was a part of her routine. She wouldn't let her daughter paint her fingernails, just in case she put her fingers into her mouth and accidently swallowed some of the polish. Nasty toxins!

My parents smoked cigarettes in the house and fed us Spam. I went through high school wearing bell-bottom jeans and clogs. And my dad painted giant hippie daisies on my car because I asked him to. I wrote bad poetry and song lyrics on my bedroom walls. All these things added up to me being a real, free-spirited hippie in Union County, North Carolina. I quickly learned that a wannabe hippie girl in rural North Carolina is no match for a real deal hippie in urban California. You could say our friendship never really got off the ground. Actually, you could say she couldn't stand me. She saw me as prissy, a total conformist, and a giant square. And I definitely wasn't good enough for her brother.

With my relationship with Sister over before it began, circumstances were at the breaking point. One afternoon, I returned home from work. Zach wouldn't be home for a few more hours. I climbed the two flights of stairs to the apartment and opened the door to see Mom chasing the roommate around the apartment with a knife. It wasn't a regular little knife, oh, no, but a butcher knife. Through the living room, into the kitchen, and back into the living room they went, round and round, with her screaming all the while.

It turns out the roommate had been cleaning the kitchen and threw out half a can of soup Mom had made for the half-brother. That was it for the poor roommate, death by desire for cleanliness. I assume the roommate must've talked his way out of harm's way. He's still alive, and I never heard a story of Mom's stint in the big house.

I'm not sure if being poor made her crazy, or if being crazy made her poor. Maybe that line is really blurred, and we'll never know which came first. But the one thing I did know, as I quietly backed out and shut the door, was that my time in California had come to a close. I wasn't tough enough to survive this new land. California had bested me, and once again I made the humiliating and defeated trek home to Mom and Dad. Zach begged me not to leave him, but in the end he reluctantly drove me to the airport and tearfully put me on a plane.

After I left, Zach wrote to me every single day. This was before emails and text messages, so he handwrote something every day. And he called ... every single day. He was intent on wooing me back to the West Coast.

The disdain my mother felt for him grew with every phone call and letter. She had decided that he was the devil— a selfish, controlling devil, hell-bent on destroying my life. In her mind, if he had any decency at all, he would have put me on that plane and let that serve as our breakup, never to see each other again.

I don't think she gave any credence to my heart or desires or the fact that I really did love him. How could I not? He had nothing to offer except all the things I so desperately wanted to be offered: independence and an escape from North Carolina. I wanted to be fearless, to do something besides stay in Monroe all my life. Zach was attractive and capable and offered exactly those things, particularly in the form of a plane ticket back to Berkeley. He promised to get me out of his mother's house. I asked him to take me out of Berkeley altogether.

Right after my return to him, we drove to Portland, Oregon, and took a look around. It seemed perfect to me— none of his wacky family members and nowhere close to North Carolina. Sold! We found an apartment and put a deposit down. I applied to college and was accepted. Finally, for the first time since the night I discovered I would be sleeping on a bloody futon mattress, I felt hope. Our future might turn out OK, and we might yet become the people we had hoped when we were younger and dreamed of such things. We went back to Berkeley to keep working and save some cash until it was time to move. I could deal with Mom and Company for three months, as long as I was working toward something.

During our time apart, Zach and I both slept with other people. We were young and free-spirited, so neither of us was even slightly angry with the other.

I met his little side project after my return. I don't remember her name, but I remember I liked her, and, oddly enough, she became my friend. She took me to the movies and taught me that butter tastes delicious on a saltine cracker.

She was a poetry student at UC Berkeley and had a really great basement apartment in someone's house. I was going bananas being back at Mom's, so this girl offered to sub-let us that little apartment while she went overseas for a semester of school. I could not have been more thankful.

Zach and I moved our stuff over and began to feel like we were truly settling in to a life of our own, one we were making for ourselves. From there, everything seemed to happen fast. After only a few days, maybe a week, the upstairs landlord came down and told us we had to leave. Our nameless friend had already left for another country, and we didn't know how to contact her. We had absolutely no recourse. We had to move out.

I was beyond crushed. There was no way I could go back to Mom's house. I must have sat on the couch in that strange apartment and cried forever. I called my own mom and cried and cried. And then my mother did something strange and remarkable. It was Christmas time, and she offered to buy two Greyhound bus tickets for us to come home and enjoy Christmas with family. The remarkable part was that even though my parents were flat broke, couldn't stand Zach, and disapproved of my choices, they chose to help me see my choices through. The bus tickets were round trip. They only wanted me to come home and let them love on us both for the holidays. They wanted to find a way to give us a little money to send us back out West to try our hand at Portland. As a mother now, I can't imagine the grace and restraint it must have taken for my parents to come to that decision. Of the long list of graces my parents have shown to me, this was one of the most generous.

We spent four days on that bus, passing through every one-stoplight town across the Southwest and beyond. We took a little pot with us and would get stoned behind the bus stations sometimes, just to make the obnoxiously loud and generally miserable trip a little more bearable.

Mom and Dad picked us up from the bus station on the fourth day. They were genuinely thrilled to have us home for the holidays, and somehow they even managed to be kind to Zach. We had a nice Christmas, really, we did. That whole Christmas week felt like a refuge from the bad choices I had made over the past six months. It felt like a time out, like none of the stupid shit I had pulled was real. The back and forth, East Coast to West Coast. The sum total of the six months added up to prove just how much I couldn't take care of myself. I don't mean in a keep-a-roof-over-my-head, make-sure-there-is-food-in-my-belly kind of way. I mean that I wasn't making healthy choices that would serve my life well. At Mom and Dad's that week, I felt bankrupt and incapable. I think part of me just wanted to hide in their house, forever. But I'm really stubborn, remember, so I was determined to make it to Portland and give this thing one more go.

On New Year's Eve 1997, Zach and I drove into Charlotte to celebrate. I wasn't old enough to drink yet, but we found a restaurant/bar with a live band open to those eighteen and up. At midnight, we kissed and toasted with our sodas to 1998 being a better year. We actually said out loud to one another that there was no way 1998 could be worse than 1997. Yes, we said that out loud.

The very next morning, I woke up feeling so odd. My breasts hurt. A lot. I could barely put on my bra. That had never happened to me before, never with my time of the month. This was a new, strange experience but, somehow, for some reason, I knew deep down what it meant.

That night we were driving back into Charlotte to have dinner with some friends. We canceled and decided to go to dinner alone. On the way, we stopped at a drug store and bought a pregnancy test. The drug store didn't have a public bathroom, so we walked next door to the Subway sandwich shop and went into the bathroom together. I peed on a stick and within two minutes my life had changed forever.

We quickly made a plan to not go back out West. We would return to Charlotte, and Zach would get his old job back. His bosses loved him so much. It was a local business, not all corporate-y, more like a family. They would take care

39

of us, we said, and they did.

My parents didn't take the news well. There was a lot of screaming, crying, cussing, and let's not forget the name-calling. My mom had my brother when she was sixteen, and all she wanted in this world for me was anything other than that. Even though I would be twenty-one when Noah was born, Mom didn't see this as any different than the mistakes she made. Looking back now, it wasn't.

A couple of days after we found out, I wasn't sure what I wanted to do. I knew I could never have an abortion. That just felt awful, wrong, and selfish. It wasn't the baby's fault that I was a screw up. When I told Zach that I wanted to discuss our options, he went ballistic. He told me there was no way I was aborting this baby, and I told him he was right, there was no way I was aborting the baby.

"Well, what options do you mean then?" he asked. I wanted to consider giving the baby up for adoption. We were technically homeless and literally had fifty dollars between us. We were unemployed, twenty years old, and not married. Becoming parents did not seem to me the responsible choice. Oh, and not to mention that my life as I knew it and as I had dreamed it would be was over. Forever.

Zach remained overly agitated and informed me that if I chose to give the baby up for adoption, he would wait in North Carolina for me to have the baby, and then he would take the baby to California and raise him or her there. I was driving when he said those words to me, and I don't know how I managed to not have an accident. I felt as though the wind had been knocked out of me, as if my choices had been taken from me. I was still desperately in love with Zach, and now I wasn't just choosing whether to have a baby. I was choosing whether I was going to let what I thought was the love of my life walk right out of my life. Plus, I couldn't let him take the baby and then spend the rest of my life knowing exactly where my child was but deciding to ignore him or her and go on with my life. What kind of person would that make me? I felt like attempting to live my life out that way would turn me into a monster.

As we sat in the car, everything shifted for us. I began to resent Zach for giving me that ultimatum. I learned right there that we were not a team. We weren't really in this together. We were just two kids who had a hot and steamy love affair and made a baby. Now, we were going to do the best we could not to fuck the rest of this up. All these years later, I will say that we tried damn hard and did a whole lot better than I would have thought two stupid kids could have done. I'm so sad for all the awful parts, and there were plenty of awful parts, but we could have done far, far worse than we did.

Zach's bosses loaned us the money to rent a studio apartment and even gave me a job in their central office. My parents eventually calmed down, although Mom did vacillate between pressuring Zach and I to get married and then making sure I knew I didn't have to marry him if I didn't want to. I did want to but he didn't seem to.

One day in March, I think, we were at home, and I was emotionally spiraling out of control because I was so afraid of what would become of my life. I ran outside and sat down on the sidewalk in front of our apartment, bawling my eyes out, and Zach came out to sit with me. The only solution the poor twenty-one-year-old kid could come up with to calm me down was to ask me to marry him. Yep, right there on the sidewalk as I cried because my life was over. There was no ring or getting down on one knee. There was no speech about how he couldn't imagine living the rest of his life without me. There was only panic because this girl he'd knocked up was losing her mind and he didn't know how to stop it. So he proposed. How romantic.

We were married in June. I was eight months pregnant, and it was over 100 degrees. The whole wedding couldn't have cost more than $1,000. At a head shop in Charlotte called "Infinity's End," we bought plain, simple, silver bands for maybe fifteen or twenty dollars each. They were perfectly displayed right between the bongs and the rolling papers, next to the Grateful Dead skull earrings. Those were our wedding rings, and we never replaced them, not even when we were doing better financially.

Sometimes, the hardest thing to do is to be honest with yourself. But here's the truth: I never got excited for this baby. I never wanted him. I didn't want this life. I felt trapped and was certain I would fail simply because I was too young to know what I was doing.

Ani DiFranco's song "out of habit" mostly got me through my pregnancy. I got in the car day after day and cried as I screamed these words:

> i don't want to play for you anymore
> show me what you can do
> tell me what are you here for
> i want my old friends
> i want my old face
> i want my old mind
> fuck this time and place

Grief comes in so many different forms. It is certainly the death of a loved one. But it is also the death of a dream, or many dreams in my case. Grief is also learning to let go of the disappointment of all the things you missed out on. I didn't get a proper proposal. I didn't get to feel special and wanted as someone's love and partner for the rest of their lives. I was proposed to because I was knocked up and it was the right thing to do. I didn't plan a beautiful wedding and had showers and a bachelorette party. I never got to talk and decide with my husband when we wanted to start a family or felt the excitement of trying to make our baby. I never took a pregnancy test praying and hoping it would be positive. I didn't get to plan the perfect way to tell our families and have them all go crazy with excitement at the good news. And I certainly never got to spend hours laying in my husband's arms, dreaming about what our family would be like and what kind of parents we wanted to be. Instead, we just did our best to survive. I mourn all of those losses.

CHAPTER THREE
FUNNY THING ABOUT DREAMS

When I was a little girl and then a teenager, all I thought about was going to college. One semester, when I was in the fourth grade, we had a student teacher from Wingate University. She was so old (to us) and cool and pretty. And she was smart, obviously, or they wouldn't have let her come and teach little kids. I couldn't wait to be old enough to do wonderful and smart things just like her. I didn't want to teach elementary school, but I wanted to go to college and learn everything in the world there was to learn.

I think every person, when they're little, has some sort of dream of how their life will go. The world is big and full of opportunity. I doubt there has ever been a child who says, "You know, I think I want to wait tables my whole life," or, "I think working in fast food for the rest of my life sounds exhilarating!" No, we think more of becoming astronauts, doctors, or missionaries. Then, as we become teenagers and head toward college, we fine-tune that a little to social workers, interior decorators, or teachers. Regardless, we all have dreams, and it's devastating when we reach a time in our lives where the dream circles the drain and flows down into nothingness.

No one in my family had ever graduated from college, and I was determined to be the first. It was my one and only dream. I wasn't sure what I would major in; I'd figure that out once I was there. But I knew I wanted to graduate, work for a while, get married and have some babies, then go back to my career when the kids were older. This is not a mind-blowing dream. I understand that it's pretty standard, but it was a real diversion from the path people in my family had always taken. Most of my family spent their lives reacting to whatever the world threw their way, or simply did not engage their lives at all. I planned to be very different, to be proactive, to plan the life I wanted, and then go out and get it. I wouldn't let life catch me by surprise. No, sir!

When I found myself making one poor choice after another and felt my life beginning to unravel at the seams, it totally upended me. How did I get to twenty-one, married and raising a baby, with no college education?

It happened so fast, a blink and a blur, but there I was, nonetheless. It turned out that I was quite good at being a mommy. I have just enough OCD in me that I loved putting Noah on a schedule and doing housework and grocery shopping. This was right before the Internet became a thing, so I didn't have a thousand articles to read and an endless supply of other mommies to compare to myself to.

I only had one friend, Christine, who'd had a little girl eight months before Noah was born. She had been Zach's boss, and long before California we had gone to her and her boyfriend's house once for dinner. She served caprese salad and rare tuna, both things I had never had before. She still makes fun of me for how I tried to turn my nose up at her new and strange offerings and because I didn't know to squeeze lemon on my fish. After Zach and I returned, he visited Christine, knowing she was in the final month of her pregnancy. He told her and her boyfriend I was pregnant and that we were back in Charlotte to stay. Sometime after her daughter was born, Christine began to call me. I thought it was so odd and slightly uncomfortable. I had only met this woman once or twice. She was a few years older than me, and I couldn't fathom why she was would take such an interest in some young, pregnant girl she barely knew.

But throughout my pregnancy, she just kept showing up. I started hanging out at her house and slowly learned how to be a mom. She was really good at it. She made homemade baby food, rarely feeding her daughter anything out of a jar. She used cloth diapers and was a champion at breastfeeding. I had never seen anyone breastfeed before. And she became my friend, my dear lifelong, sister-like, friend. After Noah was born, she would come pick me up and take me to the mall, so I could get out of the house for a while. I didn't have a very good stroller for Noah, so she would put her daughter in her Baby Bjorn and let me put Noah in her stroller. She made parenting looks effortless and made being my friend seem like an honor. I grew relaxed and comfortable with my new role as a mom by watching the ease with which she handled it. She took me under her wing, and Noah and I have been thankful ever since. Most of all, she taught me to just love Noah the best I knew how, to make sure he was clean and fed, and to read to him all the time.

While I adjusted to my new life fairly well, those childhood and teenage dreams were now dead in the water. Even with that precious little boy smiling at me and sleeping on my chest every afternoon, this was not the life I had chosen. There was no one to blame but myself.

So, I did the only thing I knew to do. I made up new dreams. I allowed myself to hope for new things. No matter how off course our lives get or how depressed we become, we can keep going as long as we have something to hope for. I wasn't ready to resign myself to a pit of despair. Not yet.

Handsome husband? Check. Sweet little baby boy? Check. Stay-at-home-mom? Check. Rather than going for my college degree, Zach and I decided to focus on growing our little family. In an ideal world, we agreed that we would like to have three children, and, hopefully, they would all be boys.

I was terrified of raising girls. I knew what a terror I was and how rough my relationship with my mom had been—so, no, thank you! I had no desire to sign up for any of that. Plus, there is absolutely nothing feminine or girly about me, and I'm sure I would have had a girl obsessed with pastels and accessorizing, and then I would have to give her back. Or, I could drop her off with one of those pageant moms and let her raise the girl. Either way, I was certain having a girl wouldn't turn out well for me.

Just like most couples, and probably even more so because of the circumstances surrounding how we got married, our relationship ran into hard times. We were so young and had no friends or older couples to guide us or any kind of support, really. That being the case, I'm pretty proud of how we managed, but that's not to say it didn't get rocky as shit, sometimes.

Zach needed to fill every role in my life because, other than Christine, I was alone. I needed him to be my husband, lover, co-parent, provider, and best friend—all at once, from six to nine every night. That poor man would go to work at five or six a.m. every day and not get home until six p.m. By the time he returned, I was so lonely and in horrible need of affirmation that he could barely get in the door before my expectations started to wash over him in waves. It's a miracle I didn't drown him altogether.

Back then, Zach had a bit of a temper, and he didn't control it all that well. When the forces of my loneliness and his feelings of not being enough for me collided, it made for one explosive cocktail. Screaming and tears characterized the first year or so of our marriage. To this day, I never doubt our love or devotion to one another back then, even with all that turmoil. We were just young and afraid and didn't know how to do any better.

I believe deep down that I was the one who made our marriage hard. I'm the one that drove Zach away and created a space that he found utterly impossible to meet me in. But, eventually, I was also the one who decided to leave him for a time. Noah and I stayed with my parents for a season. It was the right call, but looking back now, I wonder if it wasn't a little shortsighted to assume the problem was Zach's temper and his inability to meet every need I set before him. Did my neediness and inability to find creative ways to satisfy those needs contribute to his anger just as much as our shared disappointment in the life we had accidently made for ourselves?

Zach courted me while we were apart. We went on dates, he brought me gifts, and we talked out all the things that were tearing us apart. Loving one another was never our problem. Our time away from each other began to feel like a characterization of our entire relationship, first when I came home from California and went back, and now this. We were consumed by fits and starts. Had I been ten years older, I may have recognized a dangerous pattern there and decided to quit while we were ahead, but at twenty-two, I believed that true love conquered all.

Unlike Zach's parents, mine were still married, despite their relationship having often been intensely tenuous. That was the example set before me, and I believed deep in my bones that divorce was never an option. Mom and Dad had never once forced that value on me. I merely adopted it somewhere along the way.

After three months I went home. Zach and I had fallen back into a deep connection and longing for one another, and I must have thought I had been gone long enough to prove my point. Even though I had no desire or intention to divorce, I needed Zach to believe I was strong enough to make that choice if I felt I had to.

Once we were back under the same roof, we decided first thing that it was time to try for baby number two. The plan worked. For nearly two years, our marriage was lovely. The insane fighting stopped; the courting continued; and the connection remained. We were patient with each other and showed extraordinary grace at a time when I don't think we knew what grace meant. I cooked dinner and was thankful when he was home. That was it. Simply thankful with no strings attached. I found some outside interests and made a friend or two, so that released some pressure. Zach seemed to delight in me, and we were both excited for the new little life growing in my belly. I think when a marriage is so strained that you separate for three months, the best thing to do the minute you get back together is *not* to get pregnant. What we did was a gamble, and I'm grateful it worked.

Zach and I created a new dream. When I became pregnant with Zyler, I truly wanted my new life and looked forward to raising my boys. I felt a genuine sense of hope, adventure, and fulfillment.

Sadly, I have no idea when or where I got pregnant with Noah, but I know precisely the moment I did with Zyler. One of the reasons Zach and I began to treat each other more softly and kindly was because we had made a real choice for our lives for the first time since we'd found out we were pregnant with Noah. Becoming parents and spouses felt like being caught up in a wind tunnel that seemed to happen completely outside of our control. It all just went so fast. But now, for what felt like the first time, we were sitting down and deciding what we wanted and choosing the direction of our lives. It was exhilarating.

My parents didn't quite respond the same way. I thought for sure this time around it would be all smiles and congratulations. I thought Mom and Dad would be thrilled to be getting a new grandbaby to love and spoil. But they could see my dangerous pattern. I understand that now, but in that moment, the one where I proudly announced I was pregnant and their faces fell instead of giving way to huge grins, a little piece of my heart shattered and has yet to recover.

Noah's birth was not all I had hoped for. I was young, the first among my friends to have a baby, and completely uneducated about childbirth. There was no Internet and *What To Expect When You're Expecting* can only get you so far. My mom was not full of tips and advice. She was the kind of woman who believed that you went on with life as usual with the only difference being that a person was growing in your body. When the time came, you went to the hospital, did whatever the doctor said, and a couple of days later you came home with a baby.

Zach and I were flat broke when we found out about Noah, so I had government assistance for prenatal care. Down in Monroe, where my parents lived, we found a doctor who accepted Medicaid. With no research, no interview process, and no recommendations, we made an appointment with her.

It is astounding to me now to think of all we just accepted then, no questions asked. Why didn't we look for a doctor in Charlotte where we lived? Why make the drive to the next county for every visit? How did I not know to look into this doctor and find out even one thing about her?

I was desperately against having a C-section. Years after Noah was born, I found out that this doctor had a C-section rate of 90 percent. Why didn't it occur to me to ask about her position on them to try to gauge the likelihood of my having one? Her office was always crowded, and even with an appointment, I often waited more than an hour to be seen. But, still, I never thought of getting a different doctor. That decision will always haunt me.

Noah was due on Tuesday, August 25. The Friday before, Zach and I went in for our last checkup before the baby came. I was gigantic, having gained sixty pounds because I had no idea that I wasn't supposed to eat anything and everything I wanted while pregnant. The doc said she needed to see if the baby was breech. That sounded reasonable, and I figured she would do a quick ultrasound to find out. Instead, this quack doctor stuck her hand somewhere it had no business going, particularly when I was nine months pregnant.

After I experienced a flash of intense pain, she removed her hand and informed me that Noah was indeed breech. Just like that, we would need to do a C-section. Zach and I were just young and clueless enough that we took what she said as gospel. The doctor knew exactly what she was doing; her entire patient list was made up of low-income, under-educated women who didn't know better, women who never questioned what she told them. Women like me. C-sections are actual surgery, so obstetricians make more money. There are even some OBs who prefer them because they can schedule them and avoid waiting around for labor. At twenty-one, I wasn't aware of any of this.

The doctor asked if we wanted to have our baby that very afternoon, and we told her, "Of course not!" because we hadn't packed our bags or anything, yet. We scheduled the surgery for the 24th, and I left feeling so disappointed.

Noah arrived Monday night at 8:50 p.m. Even though we had been there for hours, the doc was running late, meaning I wound up with a spinal block instead of an epidural. The operating room nurse, Buffy, who had giant breasts, made me sit up on the side of the OR table, lean over, and rest my head between those big ol' boobs. She said I had to be very still because spinal blocks are more risky than epidurals. I was so terrified, I barely let out a breath.

As the surgery got underway, I could feel myself beginning to throw up. Fearing that I was about to choke to death on my own vomit, I told the anesthesiologist. He sweetly and gently assured me not to worry, that he was going to take care of it. That's the last thing I remember because he "took care of it" by putting me to sleep. I woke up already in my own room, surrounded by my family. Everyone in the world had held my baby before I'd had a chance. I could not have felt more crushed.

When it was time to find an OB/Gyn for my second pregnancy, I was determined not to make the same mistakes. I wanted a beautiful experience full of sweet memories. By that time, Christine had two daughters, and she adored her doctor. She had told me details of her birth experiences, and this man sounded exactly like what I wanted. His name was Dr. Kopczynski, but his patients called him Dr. K.

Christine was right, and I fell in love with Dr. K right away. His presence was calming, but he was quick to crack fantastic jokes. He never rushed through my appointments or seemed flustered with my endless questions. And his demeanor was just such that I knew I was in good hands medically.

For some reason, having a C-section with Noah had left me feeling like less of a woman. I knew that I had carried the baby, but women's bodies are meant to have contractions and go into labor on their own. We are meant to have our water break, to count the number of minutes between contractions, and feel what it's like for our bodies to do the things that only they can do. I felt cheated and, honestly, a bit inferior. I wanted a good birth story, one to be proud of. It was a relief when Dr. K said that as long as I stayed healthy and the pregnancy went well, he saw no reason I couldn't have a VBAC (vaginal birth after cesarean). He knew how important it was for me to experience childbirth the way women have been doing it for eons.

Zach and I began attending The Bradley Method® childbirth classes. The classes focused on natural childbirth and how to go through the entire process without drugs. I was intent on having a natural birth and did my very best to correct every mistake I'd made with Noah. I read everything I could get my hands on, didn't skip a single childbirth class, did my Kegel exercises, ate better, and had a damn fine doctor this time. I felt empowered and encouraged. I was so happy to be pregnant and was ridiculously happy that I was happy.

Sometime in the summer of 2000, Zach and I went to the doc for my eighteen-week checkup and the ultrasound that would tell us the sex of the baby. We were so excited we could barely stand it. Of course, we said what all parents say: "We just want a healthy baby. We'll be thrilled no matter what." Honestly, we fiercely wanted a boy. I can still vaguely see the inside of that room and feel the things I felt laying on that exam table. The ultrasound technician was a woman, and "It's a boy!" rang in our ears for long after the words left her mouth. But then her face changed. She twisted her lips and squinted. She needed to go speak with Dr. K, she said, and she would be right back. But she didn't make eye contact with us.

The tech never returned. When the door opened again, Dr. K walked in to explain what the ultrasound revealed. I had something called *placenta previa*, which is pretty common. That simply means that my placenta was laying over my cervix. Many times over the course of a woman's pregnancy, as her belly gets bigger, the placenta moves up, thus unblocking the cervix. That didn't sound so bad.

"So, I can still have a vaginal birth, provided that my placenta does move up, right?" I asked.

Dr. K answered: "Well, that isn't the only thing going on in your belly. You also have something called *placenta accreta*. Your placenta and uterus have grown together." There was no way I could have a vaginal birth or carry this baby to term. He continued: "Eventually, we'll have to put you on bed rest for the remainder of your pregnancy, because the larger your stomach gets, the more likely it is that your placenta will tear away from your uterus, causing you to hemorrhage. At a later time, we'll determine how early to schedule your C-section."

I was pretty sure a bomb had just gone off in that room. I didn't understand why everyone wasn't running for cover, because I was certain the world had just come to an end.

"There's one more thing, Blake," Dr. K said, interrupting my feelings of impending doom. "Once I get the baby out, I'll have to separate your placenta and uterus. Sometimes, the two are too entangled for me to do that safely, and I'll have to remove your uterus altogether. I'll do everything in my power to save it, but you need to begin to prepare yourself for that possibility."

And that was it. All of my hopes and dreams and hard work for a good birth story evaporated, snatched right off the very exam table I was lying on. I was having another C-section, and this one could very well kill me.

Zach and I had driven separately because he was coming from work. He kissed and hugged me, tried to assure me that everything would be all right, and then he left. Noah was with my mom, so I drove to her house.

The world felt different now. My body felt different; it was my enemy, and in so many ways I began to hate it. But it also felt fragile and delicate.

I got out of my car at Mom's and suddenly was afraid of walking. If one of my steps landed just a little too hard, would that jostle things around too much? Would that cause me to start bleeding? How careful did I need to be, really? What was the likelihood that my baby would die?

Dr. K had assured me that my condition was more dangerous for me than for the baby, but I was skeptical. I already lived with the belief that anything and everything that could go wrong for me typically did. I had no faith this whole ordeal would turn out any differently.

And we already had some hurdles to overcome. When the time came for me to go on bed rest, someone would have to care for me, and Zach couldn't exactly quit his job. After that fateful appointment, even though my bed rest hadn't started yet, I wasn't allowed to do much of anything. I wasn't supposed to pick up Noah, who wasn't two years old, yet. Explaining to a toddler that "Mommy can't pick you up," doesn't go over very well. So, we decided to move closer to my parents because we couldn't think of another solution to safely see us through the next few months.

Dear Zach. That man was a machine and a rock. Over the course of a couple of days, in the heat of the summer, Zach rented a moving truck; went to our house in Concord; packed up every single thing we owned; and moved it all by himself to our new, little house in Wingate, just five minutes away from his in-laws. Some would call that near saint-like behavior. I don't know that I would disagree.

We had a couple of months or so in that cute, little house before Dr. K said it was time for bed rest. I was able to nest a little there, setting up a room for Noah and one for Zyler. Thankfully, I was able to be a part of Noah's second birthday party before I had to be flat on my back, unable to contribute a single thing to my family. And then, before I knew it, it was time.

Every morning, Zach would get Noah ready for preschool and feed him breakfast. Then, he would leave for work, and my dad would come over to take Noah and me to his house. My mom, a preschool teacher, took Noah to work with her. I always loved Mom's job and the folks she worked with, but at this point, her job at a wonderful preschool felt like absolute Providence.

Once they were out the door, I took up residence on the couch where I could be found until Zach got off work and picked up Noah and me. I wasn't allowed to so much as get up to make myself a sandwich, so my self-employed dad babysat me all day. He made me breakfast and lunch every single day.

Everything about me felt like I was an invalid and a burden. Dr. K sent me home from one of my checkups with a shower chair to place in my bathtub. Mercifully, he allowed me to shower daily, but only if I promised to sit on that chair. It isn't easy to feel like all you do is take up space in this world while contributing nothing to it.

It's hard to spend seven weeks telling your son over and over that you can't hold him, put him to bed, or play on the floor with him. His precious, big ol' eyes show that he doesn't understand, and you watch the rejection wash over him again and again. How do you explain this to a two-year-old? Mommy's sick? You don't want to scare him. The baby in Mommy's belly is sick? Honestly, I don't remember the reason we told Noah that I no longer got off the couch.

I only remember that after Dad went out to work in his shop, I would lie on that couch and cry most of the morning. The silver lining was the FX channel's nine-to-five-weekday

Beverly Hills 90210 marathon. I had the joy of watching the entire series from pilot to finale. Brenda, Dylan, and I became oh, so close.

Dr. K decided it would be best that I not carry Zyler past thirty-five weeks. He began painful steroid injections into my hips to mature Zyler's lungs and make them ready for the world outside of the womb. After all the shots had been administered, we planned an amniocentesis to be sure his lungs were ready for us to schedule the C-section.

My sweet daddy drove me up to Dr. K's office for the amniocentesis one morning, as I wasn't allowed to drive. My dad was such a manly man. He made his living doing paint and body repair on cars and rebuilding motorcycles. In his younger days, he'd been in motorcycle gangs. So, he was tough but also terribly sweet and gentle. Although he wouldn't say it, the thought of being in the room when Dr. K inserted the largest needle in the world into my pregnant belly terrified the shit out of him.

Christine agreed to meet us there and do the handholding while Dad waited in his truck, chain-smoking. Honestly, I think Christine was more morbidly interested in seeing the size of this needle than doing something kind for my dad, but I can assure you he didn't care what got her there. He was just thankful that she came. To this day, she and I still laugh our guts out when we think of the look on Dad's face when she showed up and he was officially off the hook. *Relief* doesn't even begin to describe it.

The results from the amnio showed that Zyler's lungs were developed, and the date of the surgery was set. November 21, 2000, would be my sweet little baby's birthday.

When I moved across the country I was scared; the day I got married, I was scared; I was terrified the day Noah was born; but none of that prepared me for the fear I felt on Zyler's birthday and the days leading up to it. We were all aware that this birth could end with my death, or a hysterectomy, or be completely normal.

My mom and dad and aunts came up to the hospital to stay in the waiting room with Noah. Zach went into the O.R. with me, and I was kept awake for the whole procedure. Once the surgery began, Zyler was pulled pretty quickly from my body, but instead of bringing him to the head of the operating table so I could see him, they immediately took him to the little examination station and began to do things to him.

You could taste panic and fear in the room. I didn't understand what was happening, and neither did Zach. He frantically began to ask for answers. Suddenly, other doctors rushed into the room to do things to Zyler. The amnio was wrong, his lungs weren't developed, and he was in trouble.

Once we realized this, I looked at Zach and asked if Dr. K had had to take my uterus out as well. Dr. K popped his head up over the little curtain preventing me from watching the surgery (thank God!) and said, "Yes, Blake. I'm taking it out right now."

How can I describe that feeling? I was loopy from the anesthesia but still capable of understanding what was happening to me, to us. I was laying on a table with my arms strapped down, my belly cut wide-open, having my dream of a third little boy removed at that very moment, while also watching my second little boy turn blue from lack of oxygen. I just wanted to go to sleep. Why wouldn't they just put some drugs in my IV to knock me out? Maybe when I woke up the whole ordeal would have been a dream.

And there was Zach, stuck in the middle of me and Zyler, not able to do anything but silently and helplessly watch and wait for our fates to be determined.

I began to hemorrhage as Dr. K cut out my woman parts, and I ended up losing more than half the blood in my body. They whisked Zyler out of the room, and I didn't know where they took him. In the end, I lost my uterus and my cervix, but I don't suppose you need one without the other, anyway. Once they had stitched me up and taken me to recovery, my blood pressure was 40/20, and my body temperature was 92 degrees.

I remember being covered in warm blankets, and Dr. K was very angry because he had ordered more blood for me and it wasn't getting to the recovery unit as fast as he thought it should. I also remember my mom and Zach being in there, even though no one is allowed in the recovery unit. I think Dr. K asked them to come in, just in case I didn't pull through. I thought that I probably was going to die and, if so, this was a lovely way to go, all covered in warm blankets and dreamy from the drugs. I was betting I would just drift off to sleep and wake up somewhere else. How nice! I was glad that Zach was Noah and Zyler's dad, because they would all be fine together.

What I don't remember is leaving the recovery unit and being taken to my own room. That apparently didn't take very long because the next thing I knew, they were wheeling Zyler into my room in an incubator and telling me to say goodbye to him. Hello and goodbye. He was being taken to a hospital with a better neonatal intensive care unit (NICU) in downtown Charlotte. I was in too delicate a state to go with him. I guess when you were almost dead an hour ago, the doctors don't think it's a good idea for you to go for a ride.

Zyler was small and had tubes in him and a little hat on his head. I reached my finger into the hole in the plastic box housing and protecting my new baby, and I rubbed his arm for the first time. And then, just like that, he was gone. Again, Zach was caught in the middle. He had no clue what to do—stay with his wife whom he thought he was losing only a couple of hours ago, or go with his infant son, who, for all we knew, might still die? We decided that my parents would stay with me and that Zach should go with Zyler.

This happened on the Tuesday before Thanksgiving. When Dr. K came to see me on Thanksgiving morning, I told him that I was going home. Of course, he told me that I absolutely was not going home. The normal hospital stay for a C-section was three days, and mine hade been far from normal. But I was persistent. I went on and on about how my baby was in the hospital—not even the same one as me—and he was hooked up to God knows what kind of machines, and I had not even held him yet, and all I wanted was to just go home and spend Thanksgiving with my family.

Dr. K finally relented. My daddy came and took me to my family's farm. My grandfather had a bed you could raise the head and the feet of with a remote control, and because it was too painful for me to lie flat, he let me stay with him for a few days. After I had rested for a couple of hours, the whole family arrived, and we had a proper Thanksgiving dinner together.

That was probably the best Thanksgiving Day and meal I have ever had. Yes, I had just had a hysterectomy and was devastated by it, but I was alive and, so far, so was my baby. Zach came to visit that evening, and he brought pictures and a Thanksgiving card the nurses had made for me. They had used Zyler's fingerprints to make the turkey on the front of the card. Inside was a Polaroid of Zach leaning over Zyler's bed. I gasped at how many tubes where running through my little boy's body. It was more shocking than I had anticipated.

Sometime in the next week, everyone had gone back to work. Noah was back at preschool with Mom everyday, and Zach was going to work and visiting Zyler at lunch and after work. I was lying in a bed, almost an hour away from my baby, trying to recover. The recovery from losing so much blood took more than I ever expected. It was a much different experience than my first C-section.

My first shower was a grand endeavor. I walked from the living room to the bathroom, climbed into the shower, bathed as fast as I could, got out, wrapped a towel around myself, and made my way back to the couch. No lotion, no makeup, no hair styling. Just washed and got out. By the time I sat down, I could barely breathe. I was exhausted and felt useless. Everyone else was doing something: working, taking care of Noah, visiting Zyler. I was just sitting and trying to catch my breath, literally.

When I finally had had all of this I could take, I decided

there was nothing to be done except go see my son. It had been only a little more than a week, but that was more than I could accept. I called Dr. K and informed him that I was driving to Charlotte to visit my baby for the first time. Back then, you weren't allowed to drive for six weeks after a C-section, and I think the doctor nearly had a coronary on the phone. In hindsight, I should have bypassed calling him and gone on my merry way. Still, Dr. K knew that when my mind was set on something, it was set. He gave me his cell phone number and made me promise to pull over and call 911 if I got into trouble, and then call him. But I made it to the hospital without any trouble.

When you first arrived at the NICU, you went through a set of doors and came to a giant sink. They had this particular soap that you had to wash your hands with for thirty or forty-five seconds. You pushed a button on the floor to turn on the faucet so your hands didn't touch the handles. Then, you walked through another set of double doors to enter the unit.

The NICU is the saddest place in the hospital. There are lots of babies there, all very sick and fighting for their lives. When you visit, you pass all the babies and see them attached to machines by tubes and wires. Of course, some of them are worse off than your baby, and you can't help but feel simultaneously grateful and heartbroken.

When I finally made it to Zyler's bed for the first time, I didn't cry when I saw him. I was too much in shock at everything they had attached to him. Zach met me there, and he was so sweet to me. He was used to it by then, so he just rubbed my back, talked to Zyler, and tried his best to normalize it for me. I was afraid to hold him, worried that I might pull out a wire or hurt him in some way. But I didn't injure him; we bonded quite well and quickly, actually. The staff said he wasn't ready to try breastfeeding, but if I brought the milk I was pumping, they would make sure he got it. The next piece of news turned our world even more upside down.

The one benefit of having your baby in the NICU is that they run every test known to man. That isn't a luxury afforded to babies born healthy. When running tests on Zyler, they found two holes in his heart. The condition is called *atrial septal defect*, ASD. They informed us that he would be fine, so long as we had the holes repaired before he began kindergarten. They set us up with a cardiologist and went on their way repairing his lungs so we could take him home.

How in the fuck had all this happened? I didn't understand. Why didn't my body work? It had almost killed Zyler and me. But now that I had my uterus yanked out, and he was going to have heart surgery, we were both going to be OK, ultimately. I guess. So, I clung to that.

Christine lived near the hospital, so for the next week I lived with her and her family. They didn't have a guest room, so Christine's husband let me sleep in the bed with her. On December 2, she was having her annual Christmas Party, which was always fun. She would make the house beautiful and cook the most delicious finger foods. Her house was filled with candles, good friends, and booze. It was part of my holiday tradition, and I didn't want to miss it that year. I needed something fun and festive to take my mind off everything.

It would be at least a couple more days before we could take Zyler home, so I spent the second week of Zyler's hospital stay helping Christine plan the party, and she drove me back and forth to the hospital whenever I wanted to go. Zyler was gradually coming off the machines, and I could stay with him for longer now. We even got to where he would breastfeed a little, though I was still pumping and bringing milk in for the times I couldn't be there.

I had rented a horrible contraption from the hospital. It attached to both breasts at once and sounded like a freight engine coming through the house. I woke up one morning at Christine's, and her friend Eric was there to repair the ceiling in the dining room before the party. I told him not to mind me; I was going into the kitchen to pump. There was no door between the kitchen and the dining room, so I just sat in a chair with my back to Eric as he worked. I'll never forget how he almost fell off of his ladder when I turned on that ridiculous machine.

"Blake, is something in there killing you?" Eric asked, genuinely startled. "Do you need me to help you?" He recently became a father, so I suppose he is familiar with breast pumps now, poor guy.

Zyler was finally released from the hospital on December 5 or 6. He was so little in his car seat. Noah was eight and a half pounds at birth. Zyler's six pounds made him look like a shrimp in comparison. However, the doctors told us that Zyler would be just fine. Outside of keeping regular appointments with his cardiologist, there was nothing to worry about. His lungs were completely healthy, and he was just like any other baby. That was wonderful to hear and hard to believe. We took him home and believed for the best, although I was constantly afraid I would break him.

During the next year, it seemed that they were right. Zyler did grow and develop just like Noah had. He ate the same amount as other children; he hit milestones, such as rolling over and crawling, at just the right developmental stages. He wasn't a sickly baby or too skinny, which was something I thought could happen with a heart condition. He was perfectly normal, happy, and sweet in every way, except that he happened to have two holes in his heart.

I know we tend to romanticize a thing once it is over and we have moved beyond it, but the year Zyler was with us really was a lovely year. Our marriage was the best it ever was, and I was in love with being a mother. My parents were easier to be with than they ever had been. I suppose two near-death experiences can change the dynamic of any relationship and that could be true of my marriage, as well.

Whatever the reason, Zach and I both would say we were happy that year. However happy we were, though, didn't take away the season of deep mourning at the loss of my uterus. I thought I had reinvented the dream for my life, but now that dream had to shift again. I was a mother of *two* boys, not three—a mother without a uterus at twenty-three years old. Losing my uterus and cervix hadn't made me feel like less of a woman, as I had feared it would. I was never that feminine, anyway. Still, this felt like one more area of my life where I had failed. The hard part was that it was absolutely permanent. I could do nothing to correct this. I couldn't concoct some new dream to overcome this loss; I was stuck here.

Sometimes, when the sadness was just too strong, I would dream of uterus transplants. I even asked Dr. K about them once during a checkup. He said he didn't think one had ever been done, so I would daydream of being the first. Or maybe we could just adopt instead? Maybe I was meant to learn to live with disappointment? I had no idea.

CHAPTER FOUR
OUR DEARLY DEPARTED

Surely, I had one more go in me. Yes, Zyler was dead, as was my inhospitable womb, but I was only twenty-four years old for Christ's sake. I still had Noah and Zach. There was still a family left standing after all the dust settled. We were barely standing—maybe more like clinging on for dear life—but we were still here, damn it! And I was determined to find a way through to something that resembled a life worth living.

The weeks immediately following Zyler's death were brutal, and somehow, over time, those days become more and more hazy and blurred. I still didn't have very many friends and no faith community, so I was mostly alone in my grief. I had a three-year-old to keep me company and busy. Zach returned to work two days after the funeral.

Ah, the funeral. During Zyler's short life, I learned that I enjoyed cheap wine and chat rooms. I had to take Zyler to monthly cardiologist appointments, and sometimes he had to take home and wear heart monitors, which always led to an EKG. I got used to the constant testing, I suppose, but it began to take a toll.

While I had never been a drinker, I now found myself going down to the Food Lion for cheap bottles of red wine.

At night, after all three of my guys were in bed, I would sit at the desk in our little office, listening to KD Lang, drinking wine and waiting on the dial-up to connect me to AOL. Sometimes, I talked to strangers in chat rooms. Sometimes, I played Hearts or Mah-jongg. But, either way, my one glass of wine eventually became two, then three, as I sat there feeling sorry for myself more nights than not.

So, on the night of Zyler's funeral, I got tipsy. I don't think I drank all that much. I just drank as fast as I could as I walked out the door of my parent's house to go to the church. We didn't have a pastor, so a friend read a prayer that she'd written, and Zach delivered the eulogy. Someone videotaped it, and we still have that VHS tape, somewhere. I've never watched it. It's strange and morbid to me, anyway, that someone taped it. It wasn't a wedding. I didn't need a videographer.

Although I still would never want to go back and relive it through a video, we did end up with some rather comical moments that night. I had thought it would be really something to get a couple of doves and release them as a symbol or some shit like that. Someone, maybe my brother, went and bought two doves at the pet store for the occasion.

After Zach finished speaking, we had everyone (well, not everyone, because we had over 200 people in attendance, but most everyone) pick up helium balloons that we had blown up. We all walked outside, someone said something sweet, and we released the balloons into the air. That wasn't very environmentally friendly, but I wasn't thinking of that. I just wanted to commemorate the evening well. As soon as we let them go, a huge gust of wind came along and swept them all off in an instant. It was surreal and beautiful in a way we could never have predicted. It truly felt like Zyler's spirit was whisked away into the heavens at that precise moment.

Then, it was time for the doves, our big finale. We wanted to end this evening with a real tearjerker. We opened their cage, inviting them to partake of the freedom that Zyler's soul was now experiencing. We waited for them to fly off into their destiny, hoping their departure would take a little of our grief and heaviness with them.

The two birds timidly left their confined space, lifted up into the air, probably not more that ten or fifteen feet, and quickly fell back to the concrete of the church courtyard.

We all learned that night that domesticated doves don't fly. We were looking for something symbolic, and we got it. I just don't know what it was supposed to mean. If nothing else, it certainly provided the comic relief we really must have needed. Two hundred people concluded the celebration of my little boy's life by laughing hysterically outside a Baptist church in Wingate, North Carolina.

The days and weeks that followed all began to run into one another. In the mornings, while Noah still slept, I would lie in bed, begging God to raise my baby from the dead. I would plead and bargain with him. I would tell him that I knew he was God and could do anything he chose. I would tell him that I was going close my eyes and when I opened them he could just have Zyler lying there in my arms.

God never granted my petition.

Sometimes, I woke up in the mornings certain I heard Zyler in the next bedroom, crying in his crib. I would throw off the covers and run in there, only to find the crib just as empty as it was the night before. I don't remember how long it was before I finally took down the crib and got rid of it, but I don't think it was very long at all. I knew these were the thoughts of a mad, desperate woman and that Zyler wasn't coming home. So, Zach and I packed up his things, gave some to Goodwill, and kept just a few special items. What we kept, we packed away in the attic. I couldn't bear to look at them, anymore.

I don't know when the anger began to set in; I can't pinpoint the day bitterness began to seep into my heart. I just know that it did. It's so subtle that you don't notice your heart turning black until, suddenly, you're so full of poison that everything around you is at risk of becoming infected. I don't know when I began to actively hate God, but that day came, too. After all that had happened in my life, I became convinced that God was the Grand Puppeteer and we were his little marionettes, just dancing around on strings for his enjoyment. Or, sometimes, I saw all the people of the world as actors in one giant soap opera, like the ones I'd watched when Noah was a baby. God spent his days in his big La-Z-Boy recliner in the sky, watching the earth below like a television screen, sometimes laughing, sometimes crying, and always entertained. And I hated him for it.

I didn't see evidence that any of this general malaise leaked out in Noah's or Zach's direction, but it must have. How could it not? I don't remember the months after Zyler's death being particularly contentious between Zach and me. If we had any big fights or blow-ups, I don't recall them now. It seems more like we were just two ships passing one another, never really connecting in our grief. If anything, I think we gave each other all the space we possibly could. In the end, it would turn out to be too much space.

We were both so intent on not letting this long road of tragedy consume us or define us that we forgot to look after one another. Zach plowed ahead with his work, looking to excel there as he always had. I went right back to trying to be the best mother I could and creating the happy home and family I so desperately wanted. I think we may have discussed adopting again as we had when I had my hysterectomy. I know that Zach wanted to make me happy, and I certainly wanted him to be happy, but it seems somewhere in all that we both forgot to grieve. I accidently became bitter, and he accidently stopped wanting to be there at all.

We had just had an anniversary in June, and it was a lovely one. I still remember the dinner we had and how we celebrated. We continued to be quite sweet and tender towards one another.

Still, one morning in the heat of that summer, we woke up and Zach turned to me and said two simple words: "I'm done."

I was so clueless as to where my own husband's heart

was that I asked, "Done with what?" For all I knew, he could have been done with his job or done with eating meat.

He answered, "I'm done with this marriage."

I spent the next several months doing my best to reverse that sentence, to make him change his mind, to make him take it back. That one, tiny sentence so wrecked me that it continued to ring in my ears for months after he left sometime in late July or early August 2002, just eight or nine months after Zyler's death.

I've always been disappointed that I didn't notice the date. I don't know why it's important to me all these years later. Noah's birthday is August 24, and I know it was before then.

At any rate, there was another woman. I'll call her Liz. Where and how they met isn't relevant. All that matters is that she was his perfect out. She was the super hippie-type. She reminded me of his sister, really. She had never been married, had no kids, and, as far as I knew, all of her reproductive organs were intact.

Liz was clearly a free spirit, covered in tattoos, wearing flowing skirts, and encouraging Zach to follow his dreams. *Carpe diem*, as it were. She adored him and gave him all the attention he so desperately needed then. I don't say that with any teeth or sarcasm. Things at home were heavy. Zach and I may not have been fighting but were more like two zombies occupying the same space and not eating one another. He did need some positive attention, and she showed up just in the nick of time.

I knew things weren't what we would hope for the long term, but I did believe that over time, Zach and I would heal our marriage and our life. Everything would be better and stronger than ever. Of all the things I was bitter about, my marriage and family weren't on the list. My family was the only thing that I thought would save me. It was the only light and hope at the end of the tunnel of this horrid and cruel world. I couldn't count on anything, but I could trust in my little family of three.

Zach's heart and mind were not in the same place. While I believed that the only thing getting me through this horrible mess was the idea of the three of us coming out on the other side together, Zach was silently languishing and wanting out more each day.

Being someone's husband and father was turning out to be more than he could carry. I think Zyler's death was the push Zach needed to realize that life had gone way too fast—and he may not have ever really wanted any of it. I hadn't wanted it, either, but we adapt, right? Our dreams change with our circumstances and choices, don't they? Zach had adapted with each new addition: Noah, a wife, Zyler. But I don't think his dreams ever changed. Now that Zyler was dead, it all came crashing down around him, and there was this new girl telling him everything he could possibly want to hear.

Zach's sister was living in Vermont, and we had planned to go up that summer and spend an entire month with her. It was all I could think about, I so badly wanted out of the city where my baby had died. While I'd never been to Vermont, the idea of lush greens and mountain countryside sounded like the cure for what was ailing me. It all had me counting down the days until we hopped in my Jeep Cherokee and took off. Zach knew how much I needed this trip, and it just added to the pain when he said he was done not long before we were supposed to go.

Would I ever get a break? Everything in my life felt as though it would fall apart. Why make any plans or have any hopes or dreams, even tiny ones like a vacation? What was the point? All of this ramped up my bitterness even more, but I was determined to win Zach back, bitter or not. I spent the next several months being a bit of a doormat, starting with letting Zach take Noah and my Jeep Cherokee to Vermont without me. I figured it was probably best to give him some space. Maybe he would come to his senses in Vermont and realize he didn't really want to end our marriage or be without me.

My little plan didn't work. None of my plans worked, and I came up with a few. He didn't come back from up North with a renewed love for me and for family. If anything, I think Vermont may have sealed the deal for him. I asked him if he had spoken with "her" while he was away, and he admitted that he had. I remember not understanding at all why he wouldn't just stop speaking with Liz. It seemed so simple to me. Leave her alone and only focus on me, and his feelings for me would eventually return. I now know how foolish that is. He didn't want his feelings for me to return, and he didn't want to let her go. He wanted a new start on his terms, a life he chose. I get that now, but I was just desperate to hold on to what I had. To lose it all now would feel like utter defeat and like all the years of hard work and sacrifice and bullshit would have been for absolutely nothing.

I wish we had the wisdom that we need in the moments we need it, but that is so often not the way, is it? It's usually walking through a thing that imparts wisdom upon you, and it isn't until years later that you look back to see the pieces of the puzzle fit together perfectly. At the time you are in the middle of the crisis, nothing seems to fit at all. Looking back now, all I feel for Zach is grace. It is so clear to me why he chose the things he did. He did it all wrong and just about as painfully as he could have, but I understand his choices. I wish I'd understood at the time because maybe losing him wouldn't have hurt so much. And I wish I could have seen myself a little more honestly, as well.

I wish I could have believed that it wasn't all my fault and that, actually, it wasn't all *her* fault, either. Yeah, Liz was pretty shitty, too. She should've left Zach alone once she found out he was married and especially once she found out that I didn't want my marriage to end. She should have walked away and given us a fighting chance. If we had decided we were done on our own terms, then she could have had him.

But Liz didn't give up. She pursued. All these years later, she and Zach are still together, believe it or not. They finally got married in 2012, ten years later. Zach married his rebound girl. How do you like that?

During those first few desperate months, I didn't behave sanely, either. When Zach returned from Vermont, I was unpacking a bag while he was still at my house, and I found nine—yes, *nine*—mixtapes Liz had made him for the drive. Do you have any idea how long it takes to make just one mixtape, not to mention nine? My Cherokee didn't have a CD player, so she sacrificed hours upon hours of her life to make sure my husband would be thinking of her all the way to Vermont and back.

When I pulled those tapes out of that bag, I went cuckoo for Cocoa Puffs. Did this stupid woman not have any idea what I had been through in the last year—or *six*? I had been through hell and back with this man, and now she was just going to waltz into my life and take him?

I marched myself outside and placed every one of those tapes behind the wheels of my car. I proceeded to hop into the car, while screaming like a maniac, and drive back and forth, back and forth, up and down my driveway, smashing those tapes to bits, as Zach stood in the yard yelling for me to calm down. I didn't care how loudly he yelled. That was the first time in a long time that I didn't feel like a victim. I needed relief. I needed someone to care for me, and if no one else would, then I would just do it myself.

That was the first of two times I came unglued in front of poor Noah and scared that child to death.

Even in the most amicable and respectful of divorces, which mine actually turned out to be, there will be moments when we embarrass ourselves. You can't help it, because when your spouse decides to divorce you, you're left with such feelings of rejection and failure, and even more so when they have already chosen someone to take your place. You can't help but compare yourself to that person and wonder what their intimate moments are like to make him prefer them to yours. I don't just mean sex. I mean staring into each other's eyes and talking about the depths of your souls. You think about this everyday that your spouse is with them and not with you. What is she giving him that you obviously never could? It's a crippling blow to your self-esteem. Couple that with all the loss I had experienced over the years, which now included losing the dream of having any family at all, and it is a flat-out miracle that I didn't act any more insanely than I did.

Zach moved out right away. He already had been staying somewhere else before Vermont. He told me it was with someone he worked with, and I believed him. It turned out he really was staying with *her* from the get go.

So after this mixtape scene, he got his own little studio apartment not far from my house, our house. When he told me he had rented it, I knew somehow that he wasn't going to come back, so I washed his dirty clothes and neatly packed all of his clothes in a bag. I went through the house, collected any of his personal things that were still lying around, and packed them into boxes. I included our wedding album. I couldn't bear to have it in the house any longer. I placed it all on the porch and asked him to come get it after work. When I woke up the next morning, it was all gone.

The second time I embarrassed myself almost to death was the first time I took Noah to Zach's apartment for the weekend. He hadn't been living there very long, and I knew he didn't have any money. He still had to pay the bills on my house because I was a stay-at-home mom and hadn't gotten a job, yet, and now he had to pay his own rent, too. Money was definitely tight. But when I walked into that apartment, it was perfectly furnished and decorated. There were pictures on the walls and dried flowers hanging upside-down next to the television, perfectly tied with a little ribbon. I thought I would puke. A woman had clearly decorated this apartment, and where had all this furniture come from? And why did everything look like it had come straight out of a Grateful Dead video? Hippies.

Suddenly, the same rage that had overtaken me with those horrible mixtapes was overtaking me again. I began to go through all of Zach's things like a deranged lunatic, opening drawers, looking behind the shower curtain, opening cabinets. And then I got to the kitchen. I opened the silverware drawer, and it was so full of silverware—far more than any one or even two human beings could possibly need.

That was it, the breaking point. The silverware did me in. The kitchen window was open, and I began to fling forks and knives out into the parking lot below, screaming something about his "fucking whore" the entire time, and all in front of Noah. How responsible and motherly of me.

I believe that incident ended with Zach physically removing me from his apartment. After I calmed down, I was so mortified at what I had done in front of Noah that I drove all over the city looking for the two of them. We must not have had cell phones, yet, and if we did, Zach wasn't answering. I drove around until I found Zach's car at *her* best friend's house. Summoning all the humility I think I have ever felt, I knocked on that woman's door, knowing that she knew who I was and that Zach had just told her what I had done. I took Noah out into the yard by myself. He was a bit nervous around me after just witnessing a side of his mother he had never seen. I cried and cried as I apologized to my four-year-old and begged him to forgive me. I apologized to Zach, too, and left.

Looking back now, though, I don't think these two incidents of absolute rage were my most embarrassing moments. At least through Christmas, I continued to beg Zach to come back to me. I held out some kind of hope that I could still "win." That's how I saw it. There would be a winner and a loser. To this day, whenever I see the episode of *Grey's Anatomy* where Meredith begs Derek to pick her over his wife, it touches a place far too close to home, only in my case, it was the wife begging to be picked.

I was fighting for so much; it wasn't just about getting the guy. I had made a decision for the whole of my life based on one moment before Noah's birth, the moment when Zach said that if I gave up our child for adoption, he would take him to California and raise him without me. I think I subconsciously held Zach responsible for everything that had come since that conversation, and now *he* had left *me*?! He had no right.

Plus, I had reinvented my dream so many times now, and every version was based on him and our life together. I was getting worn down, tired of reimagining my life. All I had left of my dream was a small family with only one boy, not three, and now Zach had taken away the family part. I was just a single mother now. A single mother with no uterus. How was I ever supposed to find another husband? I was only twenty-five years old with a dead baby, a four-year-old, an ex-husband, and no ability to have more babies.

Just like that, Zach had consigned me to Old Maid status while his life would go on just fine without me. So I had to win him back. It was the only way life would make sense and be worth living. I did the only, last, logical thing I could: I continued to sleep with him through the holidays. And that son of a bitch let me. He didn't turn me down when I offered myself as a last ditch effort, hoping what I wasn't accomplishing through my words, I could accomplish with my vagina. Sometimes, we women can be so stupid.

Of course, it didn't work, and the most humiliating moment in all of it was the day Zach told me he had confessed to *her* that he was still sleeping with me. Liz said that if he didn't stop, then she couldn't see him any longer. He told me that we would never sleep together again. He chose her. Again and again, he would choose her. For some reason, I think I was surprised each time. I know it broke my heart every single time.

Sometime around the beginning of 2003, I smartened up and realized that the best way to protect my heart was to have no communication with Zach, whatsoever. I asked that we only speak through emails, and I set up pickup and drop-off with Noah at a friend's house so I wouldn't have to see Zach. By no means did any of this heal my heart, but it did begin the healing process. I don't know when I began to feel strong enough to return to a full-fledged, co-parenting relationship with Zach, but that day did come. Slowly. Eventually.

Today, we have an amazing relationship. We talk on the phone at length about Noah and even about our own lives. I would go so far as to say we enjoy a certain type of friendship, even. It isn't awkward to be with Zach and Liz at school functions or holidays. My aunt passed away recently, and they came to the funeral. Liz hugged me and told me how sorry she was for my loss and that she loved me. I told her I loved her, too, and I sincerely do.

It often is quite hard to hold all these emotions in tension. I wish that when we were growing up in school, we were all required to take a behavioral psychology class, combined with a healthy, solid theology class. As I have become an adult and have suffered through and struggled with grief, the thing I have found hardest is living with these coexisting emotions. If only someone had taught me that I would feel everything all at once and that probably none of those feelings would ever truly go away. I would simultaneously love Zach for all the life we had lived together and hate him for all the ways he hurt me. I would love the fact that Noah is my son and be so grateful for all the ways he has changed me and, at the same time, hate that it all came into being the way that it did. I would be thankful for my memories with Zyler and that, for a short period of my life, I had a family, while also resenting that any of those things happened to me in the first place.

Now, I have to carry around all those goddamned memories, and for what? I want to find the gratitude in them, but more often than not they merely haunt me. I carry guilt and sadness over my past and still look forward to the hopefulness of my future. I feel all of this at the same time, all of the time.

I have small obsessions with films and television shows that depict strong, loving families. Every Christmas, I have to watch *The Family Stone* because it's about a family with five grown children who are all friends. Most of them have children of their own, and you see the dynamic between parents, children, and grandchildren, all woven together with a fierce love and protection of one another. Of course, there's also the show *Parenthood*, which is much the same as *The Family Stone*. Maybe I just want Craig T. Nelson to be my father, too, like he is for both of these fictional families. But the point is, I have spent more years than I care to remember pretending those were my families and that I was the mama of all those kids. I imagine family vacations and sporting events and deciding with my husband how to discipline the kids. I imagine still being married to the man who saw our children born. Every year, I wish for a Christmas where my son doesn't have to travel from one parent's house to the other and a child's birthday party where I don't have to consider the fact that the woman who took my husband away will be there.

Not long after Zyler died, my father went to the pharmacy to pick up a prescription. He must have had a friendship with the pharmacist, because he came home and told me that she had lost her son twenty-something years ago. He had told her of the loss our family had just experienced and asked if she had any advice for me. She told my dad the only thing she could say was that the pain will lessen over time, but that it never truly goes away. She said to tell me that I would carry that hurt in my heart, forever.

When Dad came home and gave me that message, I thought two things. First, how terrifying and awful that twenty years from now, this all would hurt just the same. Second, I didn't believe her. That may have been her experience, but it wasn't going to be mine. I would get beyond this, and I very much doubted that it would continue to cripple me in the next few years, much less in twenty. How naïve I was. Maybe that arrogance contributed to the void that took shape between Zach and me. Maybe it contributed to all of my unhealthy living over the next few years. Either way, it turns out the pharmacist was exactly right.

During the years following Zyler's death and Zach's exit,

I read several grief books. Each of them walked me through the stages of grief and told me what to expect. Anger and guilt were natural and normal, they said, and there would be a stage of denial. But, just like when I sat in that therapist's office in the months after Zyler passed away, I was always looking for someone or something to tell me what to *do* with the grief. Tell me how to process it, move past it, and get on with the rest of my life. I wanted so badly to put it all in a little box and—just like the crib and wedding album and Rubbermaid bin holding Zyler's belongings—store it in the attic.

After thirteen arduous years, I have finally learned that grief doesn't work that way. The pharmacist was right. I will carry this pain forever. I am ever so thankful that I no longer have gaping wounds that bleed all over everyone and every good thing in my life, but I still carry scars. I can touch them and feel the scar tissue lying just beneath the surface of my skin. Unfortunately, no amount of cosmetic surgery will remove the scars entirely. I carry them wherever I go.

I wish someone had told me back then how hard it would be to hold the tension. My life today is good and beautiful, and I really love it. It is unbelievably hard to love this life and simultaneously wish for my old one, but that's what I feel many days. It's hard to look forward to a bright and hopeful future of life and love, which is exactly what I have, and not wonder about the what-might-have-beens. It's hard not to feel insane when you are holding all of that in your heart. I wish I'd had a faith community and a smart pastor, like I do now, to teach me the heart of God for me. I no longer believe God did this to me or that I'm merely a puppet in his grand design, but back then I was utterly alone in it. Today, I believe more than anything that we were never meant to be alone. That is the one thing that will drive us to the brink of madness.

Chapter Five
God Is My Co-Pirate

"You're so strong!"

If I heard this phrase once, I heard it a thousand and one times. Let me assure you, when attempting to encourage someone who has experienced extreme loss, these are not the words they are longing to hear. Don't get me wrong, I appreciate the sentiment, and I don't mean to sound like a jerk. But let's face it, when someone is in the throes of grief, none of us know what to say—not even me, and you would think I have the perfect speech by now. I don't. I just know that no one likes to be told they're strong simply because they continue to get out of bed every morning. Well, most mornings.

Of all the junk I read about grief after Zyler died, only one story stuck with me. A mother had lost her seventeen-year-old son in a car accident. One Sunday, she was on her way out of church. As she passed the pastor, he took her hand in his and apologized for her loss. Then he said, "You know, the Lord never gives us more than we can handle."

That's when she finally snapped. She replied, "So, you're telling me that if I were a weaker person, God wouldn't have let my son die? It's because I am strong that he took him?"

So, yeah, don't tell me I'm strong. I don't want to hear

that bullshit. After Zyler died and Zach left, I didn't do one single extraordinary thing. I did continue to get out of bed. I did make Noah breakfast and take him to the park and read to him. He was bathed and loved, and I worked out a schedule with his father to be sure Noah had plenty of time with him. I didn't become addicted to drugs or sleep with every Tom, Dick, and Harry—just a couple of Toms, Dicks, and Harrys.

Eventually, I went back to work to make sure the two of us had a roof over our heads and food on the table. My parents weren't rich, and they weren't funding my disaster of a life, so I didn't have any help. I had to go to work in order to survive. Sure, I resented it. And, man, did I resent Zach. I was a stay-at-home mom. That was my vocation, and, now that there was only one child left and would ever only be one child, I wanted to soak in the last year of stay-at-home mommyhood before sending Noah off to kindergarten. But that didn't happen, either, as Zach left just in time to rob me of that one last request.

No one was going to bail me out this time, so I bailed myself out. I went to work in the deli of a health food grocery store. I can't have made very much money slinging veggie dogs and smoothies, but I had been out of the work world so long that I had to start somewhere. A husband and wife owned the store, and I found out later they were deeply Christian. They were so devout that they wouldn't allow the local, free news rag to be displayed outside the store because it contained singles ads, including some for gays and lesbians.

I felt as if I had walked into some kind of time warp, that if they knew the real me, they would never have given me a job. Thankfully, I didn't work directly under either of them. My boss in the deli was a guy in his fifties, named Wayne, who drank and smoked and cussed like a sailor, thank God! Wayne was the only thing that got me through that job. He was sent to me as a gift, all full of the salt of the earth and grit, just to let me know that I could get back on my feet. And to let me know not to ever let a curse word slip in the direction of the store's owners. I didn't work there long, maybe just a few months, but it was long enough to give me courage to know that I could do this, whatever this was. Somehow, I could take care of Noah and me. During those months, I decided to fight for some sort of future for Noah, and for myself, but mostly for Noah.

That was the beginning of the path my life took for the next five years. I worked hard at blue-collar jobs and made enough money to keep us afloat. With Noah going into kindergarten, I had to find a way to take him to school, pick him up, and still work. Ding, ding, ding! Waiting tables, you can make more money and the schedule is more flexible. Slinging pizza to uppity Uptown bankers was the perfect solution, so I left the health food store and got a job at a local pizza chain.

I don't mean to beat a dead horse, but I must go back to the "You're so strong" thing. Again, I never have figured out what about my choices folks interpreted as being strong. Had I not had a child still living, who knows what I would have ended up doing? Maybe heroin? Maybe I would have been locked up in a psych ward. But I did have a child left alive, one that I happened to love and care for deeply. Do you really think I would have done anything other than bust my ass to care for him? That isn't strength. It's called parenting. It's called love.

I can admit, though, that those five years were the darkest of my life. During Zyler's short life, I may have learned that I enjoy cheap, red wine, but at the pizza joint I learned that I loved to drink, period.

One night, not long after I had started there, I got off work and two of my coworkers were sitting at the bar drinking their nightly post-shift nightcap. They asked me to join them. That night, Eric, the uproariously funny and persnickety gay server, and Chris (we called him Big 'Ens cause he was huge), the good ol' boy cook, introduced me to the world of shots. I was on the verge of turning twenty-five, and I suppose because I left the college scene just before it was getting good, I honestly had no idea what a shot was. To Eric and Big 'Ens, I was a rarity, like purple carrots or red bananas, and they couldn't wait to school me on what all I didn't get at college frat parties.

They introduced me to Jägermeister and Rumple Minze. Shot after shot they ordered, and like a stupid kid, I drank them. It wasn't long before I no longer knew my name, where I was, or that when I came in to work the next day, I was going to have to pay—literally and figuratively—for all those shots.

These guys were the real novelty. They drank more than I did, of course, and then decided to move on to another bar. Thankfully, they agreed to take me home, or else I have no idea how I'd have gotten there. They poured me into the backseat of Eric's car, and I somehow managed to give them directions to my house. Still, Eric kept having to yell at me to "wake the fuck up and tell him where the fuck to go," or something like that.

Three seems to be the magic number of years that I like to work somewhere. For the next three years, I learned how to drink with the big boys, or the Big 'Ens if you will. By the time I left my life of pizza behind, Eric and Big 'Ens no longer out drank me, I figured out that Jack Daniel's was my drink of choice, and I finally found a way to cope with all the loss, sadness, and disappointment in my life. Cheers!

I had grown up in the same small town as another Blake. His mother was my fifth grade teacher, and, although we weren't in school together because he was ten years my senior, I knew him somehow. I guess you hear of everyone when you're in a small town. At some point, I discovered that Blake worked at a little bodega near my neighborhood, probably because my mother had heard from my aunt, who had heard from Blake's mom in Sunday school. The food in that store was yummy, so from time to time I would go there to get a sandwich and pack of cigarettes. Blake and I started up a casual acquaintance-ship over the course of my visits.

One day, I saw a sign at the checkout counter, wishing

Blake's son a happy birthday. As I was shopping, I found
Blake stocking wine and asked about his son. Come to find
out, he was born just a couple of days before Zyler. It made
my stomach drop a little, but I put on a brave face.

Blake went on to open his own little bodega called The
Common Market. It opened while I was working at the health
food store, during the "Great Ice Storm of 2002." I'm not
being funny; there really was a giant ice storm that knocked
out power for two weeks for some people, like me. Blake
opened his store stocked only with Marlboros and Coors
Light, because those were the only vendors who would
deliver in that weather.

The Common Market stayed open late, and you could
drink and smoke in there after a certain hour. In the
beginning, it was so slow and mostly empty that the few of us
who would waste our nights away in there felt like we owned
the joint. Blake wasn't there at night; his friend James worked
the night shift. Turns out, James did think he owned the place
and was giving away half the shit in the store. It didn't take
long for our nights of drinking, dancing, loud music, and
smoking to come to an abrupt halt. But before that, it seemed
like everything happened there.

I met a woman who paid her bills as a stripper but wrote
sci-fi, vampire erotica. She smoked cloves and read our tarot
cards. She was loud, obnoxious, and unlike anyone I had met
before. There were biker kids who didn't bathe and who
drank PBR tallboys. Today, they would be called *hipsters*, but
we didn't use that word in 2002.

When Noah went to kindergarten, I started at the
University of North Carolina-Charlotte. That lasted one
semester. It seems I wasn't quite cut out for single
motherhood, primary breadwinning, and college all at the
same time. Plus, I needed a social life. That booze wasn't just
going to drink itself! And, yet, during that one semester, I
managed to make a 4.0 and do nearly all of my studying at
The Common Market. I felt at home there among the
weirdos, the hipsters, the drunks and the upper-middle-class

white folk who ended up loving the store as much as everyone else. It was our little neighborhood convenience store. Over time it added a deli, a wine bar, and open mic nights.

Somehow my acquaintance with Blake turned into a friendship, which turned into a job offer. He wanted to add a juice and smoothie bar to the deli, and he asked me to head up the project. While he waited on the capital and the permits, I would work in the deli. I was so far over waiting tables that I nearly lunged across the table and kissed him in gratitude.

I worked at The Common Market for three years. They were three of the best and most fun years of my life but also the most dark and lonely. For the first time, I took pride in my work. The juice bar tanked and that was embarrassing, but I eventually moved over to the store side of the Market, instead of the deli. I absolutely loved it, and I thrived there. Over time, Blake gave me more and more responsibilities. He took great care of his employees, and it was the first time I had worked for someone I believed in. I could see myself staying there a long time, and Blake and I even dreamed of a second store and what that could mean for me. For the first time in a long, long time, I felt hopeful, as if maybe all the mistakes I had made weren't going to be the total ruin of me. I could end up with a career and a life to be proud of, even after all that had gone so, so wrong.

But I saw everything there, too. The Common Market lent itself to the most diverse group of folks I had ever encountered—well, barring my time in Berkeley, of course. I settled in to the day shift, coming in after I dropped off Noah at school. The day started at the cash register, and people would come in by the droves to get their morning coffee and a pack of smokes. Over time, I came to know all of my customers' names and stories. They treated me like their bartender and told me the details of their lives. I learned more in those three years than quite possibly any of my other three-year stints combined.

I heard plenty of scandalous stories, usually having to do with who was sleeping with whom when they shouldn't have been. One that stands out is that I had no idea we had quite a presence of swingers in our neighborhood. There were even two married couples who considered themselves all married to each other. One couple worked across the street, and they came into the store every single day. They all four slept together and went on dates in all sorts of coupling configurations.

I had the honor of hearing about successes and promotions. I was there when my regulars came in to grab some last minute booze before a wedding and when they came in to buy a sandwich and a beer after a funeral. I saw babies born and couples break up, all from behind the counter at that little store. In so many ways, it was beautiful and was the stuff life is made of.

But of all the things I saw, what surprised me most was just how sad and dark almost everyone seemed to be. Even in the happiest of times, folks wore their bitterness and cynicism on their sleeves, and it didn't do anything but feed the bitterness and cynicism growing daily in my own heart. While I loved that job for so many reasons, I think the first year or two there were my rock bottom. There was no light left in me. I no longer looked forward to a single thing. Life had become something we survive, we endure, and we get through. I existed to take care of Noah and to raise him. That was the extent of my purpose on earth. As much as I loved Noah, I wasn't able to find joy in any of it.

If someone had asked me back then if I liked my life and my job, I would have said yes. I'd say I thought things were pretty good. I made a decent living and had health insurance. I had gotten to this place on my own, and so there was some pride in that. I enjoyed my co-workers, especially Blake, and I liked the nature of my job. I was living with a girlfriend at the time, and I was dating again. By all accounts, I should have been happy-ish. But I don't know how anyone could bear to be around me for very long.

My despair and lack of hope had formed a pretty dim worldview. I've always been extremely opinionated and outspoken, so I took every chance I got to tell people that the world was a cruel and fucked up place and I wasn't sure why we all even try. I was eternally curious about the meaning of this life. What is it for? And if someone attempted to answer that question with the slightest hint of optimism, I would shut it down with talk of dead babies and philandering husbands. You could say I was a real breath of fresh air.

The funniest part was that I couldn't see any of this. I sincerely thought I was fine, just tough and hardened by this old world. I was seasoned and wise, and the world was never going to get the best of me again. My eyes were wide open now, and I wouldn't be caught unaware. I didn't see that I had become hard and rigid in ways that were hurting me.

This was a rough period for Noah, as well. He was only five or six, and even though he was incredibly smart, he was struggling with school. He wasn't getting along with his father and was behaving oddly at his house, banging his head into walls and throwing tantrums. I became increasingly concerned but was completely clueless as to how to help my son. He was his normal self at my house, and when I tried to talk to him about it, he would just say he didn't like going to his dad's.

After I had refused to continue my grief counseling back when Zyler died, my counselor, Dawn, and I became friends. During this time of Noah's unrest, I called her for advice. Noah was already seeing a therapist. Sometimes, he and Zach had joint sessions. I was being as open, verbal, and supportive with Noah as I knew how to be. I had meetings with his teachers. At home, I gave him all the one-on-one attention I knew how.

Dawn wasn't sure what else I could be doing, either, so she consulted with her boss. After she explained the entire situation from beginning to end, he looked at her and said, "The problem is that Blake hasn't addressed her depression and hurt. Noah can sense that, and it's spilling over into him, causing him depression and anxiety."

Dawn informed him that there was no way I was depressed, that I was far too high-functioning for that. Her boss answered that he didn't care how high functioning I was, no one goes through all I had been through and comes out unscathed. There isn't a closer bond, he said, than that of mother and child. If Noah was having this much difficulty, it was time for me to examine myself.

When Dawn relayed that message to me on the phone, I was so indignant that I practically hung up on her. How dare she and her boss suggest that I wasn't well? How did they—especially her boss—know? We had never even met.

While this was happening, I had two new customers at The Common Market: a man in his fifties, named Dennis, and one in his twenties, named Jonathan. They came in all the time for lunch, almost daily, sometimes together and sometimes bringing other friends. They were fun and easy to be with. They always seemed genuinely interested in me and in my life. They had learned about Noah and Jason, the guy I was dating, and they always asked about them. If they happened to come in to eat when the store was slow, they would invite me to sit and chat with them while they had their lunch. Somehow, the conversation always revolved around me. I don't know if I was just a totally self-absorbed human being back then, or if they just kept the questions coming, but either way, I knew very little about either of them.

Over time, I did come to realize how different Jonathan and Dennis were from the other people that shopped at the market. I don't think I had ever really known anyone like the two of them. They were happy, and when I was with them I felt at peace. They never came in complaining about some love interest gone wrong or how their boss had screwed them over. They never seemed put out by life or the world. They appeared to have an authentic and sincere love for the world, the people in it, and even their own lives. I couldn't have articulated all that at the time, of course. It's only in hindsight that I've been able to pinpoint the differences in them, but I was aware in those moments that they had something "other" that I hadn't encountered before.

Over the months, I also began to recognize that whatever they had, I wanted. Badly. I was so tired of being sad and hard, tired of being afraid that this was as good as life gets. I was sick of myself and what I had become; I wanted joy and to be at peace with myself, my life, and this stupid world that I hated so much. Why were these guys so different?

As angry as I was that Dawn would even hint that I was the cause of Noah's issues, I couldn't get her words out of my head. I was terribly offended that someone would suggest that I was hurting Noah in some way, seeing as everything I did in this life was for him. Yet, from the time I woke up in the morning until I drifted to sleep at night, I thought about what Dawn's words could mean. It was all I thought about. Maybe caring for Noah wasn't just about providing for him financially, making sure his homework was done, and getting him bathed before bed. Maybe his emotional and mental health really was contingent on the state of my own health. I panicked. How in the hell was I going to get well, particularly when I wasn't fully sure what was wrong with me?

One day at the market, Dennis was getting a cup of coffee, and we were chatting. I mentioned that Jason and I were going to be moving some furniture over the weekend, particularly a couple of pianos, and we needed to find a couple of guys to help us. Dennis perked up and said he could get some guys, just leave it to him.

I couldn't have been more shocked! We didn't know each other that well. I'm not sure I knew his last name. Why would he offer to help me move furniture? Everyone hates doing that. And wasn't he a little old to be moving a piano? But Saturday came, and we met at the market for our big day. Dennis brought Jonathan and another guy who I hadn't met before.

At the time, I fully hated God but clearly believed in

him. How could I have hated him so vehemently if he didn't exist? So, I may have taken a little pride in saying or doing irreverent things where the Big Guy was concerned. On this day, I happened to be wearing a neat, little T-shirt that had Jesus donning an eye patch. In the background was a pirate ship, and the caption read, "God is my co-pirate." Clever, huh? I got a big kick out of that sarcastic take on the "God is my co-pilot" bumper sticker. Apparently, everyone else did, too, because I got a ton of compliments and chuckles every time I wore it.

As we sat waiting for Jason to show up with the truck we were going to use to move the pianos, I decided it was finally time for me to be the one asking questions. I found it so odd that Jonathan and Dennis were such good friends given their age difference. I had been trying for a while to figure out their relationship to one another. Maybe they were co-workers, or maybe Dennis was Jonathan's uncle?

So, I asked, "Hey, I was wondering, how are you guys friends? How did you get to know each other?" There was a long pause as Dennis and Jonathan looked at each other for a moment. And then, slowly, Dennis said, "Blake, Jonathan is my pastor."

I felt like the wind had been knocked out of me or I had just entered some parallel universe. These guys were nothing like what I believed Christians to be. They were kind and funny. They hung out at a place like The Common Market, for goodness' sake, and never once did they make me feel judged.

My gut reaction was to cross my arms over my shirt and begin apologizing, both for the shirt and certainly for all the foul language I had used in front of them both over the course of our friendship. I love to curse, then and now. That hasn't changed.

Isn't it sad? The only thing I could think to do when I found out they were Christians was apologize for myself. Whenever Jonathan or I tell this story, it's always hilarious, and when I think back on it, it was truly funny. But there's a part of it that breaks my heart. The Christianity we all know, the one popularized by right-wing evangelicals and the Christian culture of our time, would have us believe that the appropriate response when in the presence of a good Christian man or woman, is to apologize for ourselves. Of course, the larger implication is that we should do the same when we are in the presence of the Lord—apologize for who we are.

Thankfully, that was not Jonathan's or Dennis's position. Jonathan was so kind. He laughed and laughed at me covering my shirt and assured me that I had nothing to be embarrassed about. He loved my shirt and my salty language. Nothing I had ever done or said had offended him, he told me, and I believed him.

A lot more than just piano moving happened that day. I didn't know it, but by the end of the day I had a softer, more generous opinion of Christians. I would even go so far as to say I had a newfound curiosity about them, too. I felt loved and cared for in a way I hadn't in a very long time. See, I knew everyone in that neighborhood because of my job. Everyone and their brother knew me, but not *one* person, beside, Dennis, offered to help when I needed it. And Dennis and Jonathan didn't know me all that well. Dennis heard me say I had a need, and he simply wanted to meet that need, with no agenda, no strings attached. I believe that was the first day my hard, black heart began to soften just a little.

Things got a little peculiar from there. Jonathan and Dennis continued to hang out at the market. I adjusted pretty quickly to the fact that this tall, funny, twenty-something guy pastored a church. They didn't start telling me all about the church now that I knew, and I never once asked. Neither did they take the opportunity to try to evangelize me or even invite me to church. I'll admit I was thankful. They must have sensed that I was like a feral cat; one mention of coming to church with them, and I would have run under someone's house, never to be seen again.

Sometime around August or September 2006, things

seemed to hit a breaking point with sweet Noah. Or maybe the breaking point was just inside me, and I used Noah as my excuse to do something about it.

One morning, I woke up feeling very desperate. Back then, Noah spent half of each week with Zach and half with me. It afforded me a lot of free time to go to the bar and drink. Jason, the boyfriend, and I had a local bar we loved, and they loved us. During most of the time Noah was with his father, you could find me at that bar, drinking until I was numb, until there was no dead baby or hysterectomy or single motherhood. This was the vicious cycle of my life. I worked every day, parented half the week, and drank about it all the other half of the week. It got to the point that I didn't feel like a real human any longer. The only way I can think to describe it is that I felt like a shell, an empty vessel, or maybe even a zombie. I was standing up, moving, and functioning, but I wasn't really in there.

So that morning, I was at work and I was absolutely done in. I felt as though I no longer had a soul, and I was so very worried about my little Noah. I just wanted him to be whole and happy. I stood in the back of the store stocking the wine. Never one to do anything gently or with grace, I would take a bottle out of the box and slap a price tag on it with all the aggression that had built up inside me, then place it in the proper place on the shelf. Someone watching me might have figured that I had some personal beef with those wine bottles. I'm just thankful I didn't take them to the parking lot and start throwing them, one by one, onto the pavement, just to watch them smash. As I priced the wine, I prayed.

Now, I wouldn't have called it *prayer* at the time. People who hate God don't spend much time talking to him. It's only now that I know it was prayer. It went something like this:

"I need help. I don't know what to do anymore. I've tried everything: self-help books, counseling, Buddhism (Yes, I was a Buddhist for a few months after Zach left. I didn't like it.) Nothing has worked, and Noah is a mess. I want to take care of Noah. I don't want to hurt like this, anymore. I'm miserable, and Noah's miserable. I can't live like this. I will do anything. Anything. Just tell me what to do."

This is where things got weird. As I finished saying those words in my head, I stood up to place a bottle on the shelf. At that very moment, standing at the drink cooler behind the wine shelves, was Jonathan. He was the very first thing I saw when I stood up. I knew that meant something, and I was pissed. I mean really pissed.

I desperately wanted help—really, I did—but I had standards and conditions. I wanted nothing to do with anything that smacked of Christianity or Jesus. And I was furious because I'm someone who's willing to pay attention to the signs; I enjoy a certain level of mystery and wonder in my life. Seeing Jonathan standing there at the moment I finally allowed myself to admit how bad things were and how much I wanted help, and, well, that was mysterious, indeed.

With all of my fear and pride raging inside me, I walked over to him and said I needed to talk with him. I was so nervous about what merely asking for that meant, that I think I was a little bitchy in the asking. Somehow, Jonathan knew I wasn't asking just to sit with him while he ate his sandwich, and he invited me to come to his office the next day. I've always thought that was beautiful and remarkable. I had never set foot in this man's church. He didn't know that I hated God, the same God he loved and preached about every Sunday. Yet, he invited me to spend time with him in his office having no idea what I wanted to talk about.

How many times did I think of backing out during the next twenty-four hours? I was terrified. Actually, I was afraid either way. If I went, I'd have to tell this man everything and actually let him do his best to help me. I would have to be vulnerable and admit that seeing him standing at the drink cooler the day before was a wild quirk at the very least. Perhaps it was even the sign I was hoping for—the sign that somehow this universe didn't want to destroy me, but instead give me my life back. Did I dare to believe that? And if I did back out, that would mean staying exactly the way I had been for years, desperate and searching for help because I was too damn prideful to accept the help that was offered.

I could take the quirky experience at the drink cooler as one more thing to fuel my cynicism, one more way I was like the people at the market who were so sad all the time. I could pass up finding out what made Jonathan and Dennis different and miss seeing if there was any shot I could be like that, too. Or, I could put on my big girl pants and go take the biggest risk of all: For the first time in five years, I could hope.

The church office was all hip, modern, and furnished by Ikea, a store I had never heard of. I couldn't believe it was a church office. It was supposed to be stuffy and drab, but this place was comfortable and fun and decorated in red, black, and white. Jonathan brought me into his office and slid shut a huge metal door. His office was covered in all things U2. Nothing was like I expected.

I sat with Jonathan for two hours, baring my entire soul. In the past, I had never cried when I talked about all that had happened to me. That was my protection mechanism, but as I unfolded my entire story to him, I cried and cried. Sweet Jonathan never batted an eye. He never once seemed scandalized or horrified by my life. No one had ever looked at me like that, not even when I told the story of how my baby died; Jonathan's only expressions were compassion and sorrow. He was the first person that gave my loss the weight and sadness it deserved.

My anger came out in talking to Jonathan. I didn't let it go unsaid that I was angry with God and that I blamed him for all of this. But after I finished spilling it out, Jonathan gave bad advice. At least, I thought it was. Cynical Blake wasn't going to just let this beautiful afternoon pass without some kind of snark.

After I got it all out, Jonathan asked, "Have you told God any of this?"

Now I was the one who was scandalized. I may have thought God was a real son of a bitch, but I certainly didn't think it was appropriate to tell him so! I mean, he *is* God, after all.

Jonathan took me to the Psalms and showed me where David spent plenty of time letting the Lord know how angry or disappointed he was. He showed me the Psalms of lament, mourning, and pain. There it was, right in the Christian holy texts, all the writings of people letting out their shitty feelings in God's direction. I didn't know much about the Bible, so I had no idea that it isn't all rules and God smiting people. I didn't know that there are also tales of heartbroken people and God just wanting to hold them, heal them, and love them. I didn't know.

Jonathan suggested I go home and find some time to tell the Lord what I had just told him. He said I didn't have to like God or be a Christian to have a conversation with him. Like I said, I thought this sounded like the worst advice ever and maybe just another pastor cop-out. This guy didn't know how to fix me, so he was sending me away with some dumb assignment that wasn't going to make an ounce of difference in my life. I left just as lost and frustrated as I had come, except for that look on Jonathan's face; no one had ever looked heartbroken for me before.

I don't know for sure, but I probably got drunk that night. I probably told Jason what a waste of time that meeting was, that it was a stupid straw grab, and religion is for the weak. I can't say for sure, but probably.

However, over the next couple of days—as much as I wanted it to—my time with Jonathan wouldn't leave me alone. Whatever had transpired during those two hours hunted me and wouldn't let me alone. After a few days, I found myself home alone with plenty of time on my hands. The weather was beautiful, so I opened my front and back doors. I began walking in circles, through the house, out the front door, around the yard, in the back door, and then I'd start again. There's no telling how many times I circled the house saying, "Nope, I won't do it. I will not say anything. Fuck that!" until, finally, I had thought so much about my life and what had been stolen from me that I had worked myself into another rage. Noah deserved much better than what he had gotten, and I had no idea how I would carry the broken pieces for the rest of my life.

Before I knew it, I was yelling, cussing, crying, hating, and feeling so afraid. I told God everything. I don't think I overlooked a single feeling, including the one about him being a son of a bitch and how I hated him. He got it all, and not once did I apologize for myself and my feelings.

The Lord didn't "fix" me that day, but just like when Jonathan and Dennis made my heart just the tiniest bit softer by helping me move the pianos, something about slinging every feeling I had at God softened me a little more. I remember feeling for the first time, perhaps ever, that a little light had been let into my deeply black heart. And I liked it.

About a week later, I walked into work and told Blake he was going to have to rearrange my schedule because I was no longer available to work on Sundays. He asked why, and I told him I was going to start going to church. I don't think he was any more shocked by my pronouncement than I was.

CHAPTER SIX
NAÏVE MELODY

I don't remember the first time I saw him. I don't even remember the first time we officially met, and it drives me insane. My brain is chock-full of memories and images that I would do anything to erase, but the one thing I want to remember more than anything just isn't there. I suppose that's the way it goes. We usually don't know when we are being given our greatest gifts, so we rarely are paying attention.

Many years ago, there was a sketch comedy club in Charlotte called, "The Perch." It was gloriously vulgar and inappropriate. No one was safe, and no topic was off limits, so, naturally, I loved it. I've never been a big fan of improv, so this was perfect. It was more like *Saturday Night Live*, with each bit carefully sketched out, although the actors were known to throw a little ad lib in from time to time, causing the rest of the cast to lose their composure just a bit. The crowd always loved those moments best.

The Perch was located in the heart of an up-and-coming neighborhood, and sat above an independent clothing boutique known for their eccentric selections. At the time, the neighborhood was a few years away from coming up, so it could be just plain scary. But I loved that, too. The shows were on Friday and Saturday nights at nine and eleven, and almost every show sold out. I rarely I missed one.

Because The Perch was upstairs, the line to get in would meander down a twisty, narrow staircase and out onto the street below. The room was full of couches picked up from Salvation Army or someone's dead grandma. You could smoke there and were allowed to bring in your own booze. It was a veritable wonderland of debauchery. I brought every friend I had whenever I had the chance. I even brought my parents and my brother, once. Not being people who were easily offended, they loved everything about it just as much as I did.

And that's where it happened. That little room at the top of the stairs is where I met him. I know that as I was waiting in line to get in one of those weekends, he was standing at the top of the stairs, next to the woman taking our money and stamping our hands. He was greeting people, drinking a beer, and being silly. Sometimes, if we think about a thing long enough, our brains will create a memory for us when we desperately need one to be there. Sometimes, I think I remember seeing him at the top of those stairs and remember seeing him for the first time ever, but probably my brain just made that up to pacify me.

His name was Jason, and he was one of the actors. He had gone to East Carolina University and after graduation had moved back home to Charlotte. Auditioning for The Perch was one of the first things he did upon his return. It goes without saying that he was wildly funny.

I don't know how long we spent in each other's general vicinity before I became drawn to him. There was a small dive bar across the street from The Perch, called Elizabeth Billiards, but everyone referred to it as EBs. Before, between, and after shows, all the cast and most of the audience would run over there to have a drink or five. I know I would look forward to seeing Jason perform, and I would look forward to drinking with him after.

There was someone else in the group I'll call "Not-So-Good-Guy." Somewhere in there, I got to know him, too. To this day he is still one of the worst human beings I have ever met. He was a womanizer who claimed previously to have been addicted to heroin and who may or may not have killed a man when he was younger. Oh, and he was a notorious liar. But one thing I can say about Not-So-Good-Guy is that he was remarkably good at what he did—get the ladies. Early after my breakup with Zach, he set his sights on me and made it his goal to finagle his way into my good graces.

The end of my marriage had left me feeling so discarded and thrown out like yesterday's trash, that I was willing to jump into bed with anyone who made me feel wanted. I may have known that Not-So-Good-Guy was not so good, but he wanted me. I needed to be picked, chosen, desired. He said that I was pretty, and he was so damn confident. He may have been the worst human being I had ever met, but he was also the surest of himself, and so I let him into my life for a few months.

He was my rebound guy, added to my list of terrible decisions. Nowadays I do have grace for myself even in that choice. I knew he was awful, but I knew I needed affirmation, and that was what I was using him for. I didn't want to spend the rest of my life with him; I just wanted him to tell me I was pretty and maybe some other stuff, too.

During my time with Not-So-Good-Guy, I learned that Jason was all I really *did* want in this world. We lived in the same neighborhood, just a couple of streets away from one another. He and two other guys had a house together, and it was the greatest house, not because of its furnishings or floor plan, but because it was where everyone hung out. Never a day went by that you couldn't find at least one friend (usually more) at their house drinking, smoking, and watching a ballgame, or whatever. After spending so much of the last few years without any close friends, much less a whole group of them, I relished every opportunity to spend time at 2055 Shenandoah Road, or 2055, as we called it. Forever that house will be etched into my heart, so much so that I often talk of getting those numbers tattooed somewhere on my body. I should stop talking about that and just do it, already.

Night after night, Not-So-Good-Guy and I would go to 2055 and hang out on their front porch. We drank beers, smoked cigarettes, and listened to music. Other friends would come and go. It felt like a little family to me at a time when I very much needed not to be alone. Eventually, I realized that while all those people were great and it was certainly nice to have some company, the real reason I went there every single time that Not-So-Good-Guy suggested it was because it meant I could be near Jason. Those boys would stay up late into the night, shooting the shit and telling dumbass jokes. Even if I had to work the next morning, I never once told Not-So-Good-Guy that I was ready to go home. I would just leave them on the porch, go into the living room, and fall asleep on the couch. Just sleeping on Jason's couch was enough for me.

Jason had a friend named Laura, whom he had known since high school. She was a part of the 2055 gang, and we became fast friends. I suppose she was the first real girlfriend I made after Zach and I split. For months, we deemed every Wednesday night "Girls Night." We'd go to Thomas Street Tavern for dinner, and she would have a couple of beers, I would have a couple of Jack Daniel's, and, most important, we would pine over the men we wanted but couldn't have.

I was still seeing Not-So-Good-Guy, though I couldn't stand him. (He said I was pretty, dammit!) She wanted her old boyfriend back, but he didn't seem to be having any of that. Once Laura learned that it was really Jason who I was hopelessly in love with, she would often call him to say we were at the tavern having drinks and he should join us. Thank goodness for good girlfriends. I took every chance I could get just to be near that man. After I finally let go of Not-So-Good-Guy, Laura and I came up with other ideas to get me closer to Jason.

Many a night hanging out at 2055 Laura and I would

"accidentally" drink too much and not be able to drive home. Whoops! Every time Jason would offer to let us both come sleep in his bed with him, and Laura always made sure I got to sleep in the middle. I would snuggle as close to him as I could, content just getting to be that near to him. And every time, Jason was a perfect gentleman. He never laid a hand on me, never said or did a single inappropriate thing. It made me love him even more, although I would have given just about anything for at least one kiss.

Jason and I had a crush on each other for close to two years before we ever did a thing about it. We had a first kiss early on, before he knew about Not-So Good-Guy and me. When he found out I was seeing him, I think my stock tanked, because Jason knew what a shithead that guy was. I'm sure it caused Jason to question my judgment in general, as it should have.

I know, I know. Why would I go on to date the shithead if I had already had a kiss with Jason? I may have a long list of poor decisions under my belt, but once in a while, even I got it right. This was all happening so early after my marriage ended, and everything with these two boys seemed to be going fast. This was when I had just started working at the health food store. I was so broken and hurt and knew that I was a mess. I wasn't well, and I had no idea how much damage had been done to me.

Now, this is possibly the worst thing I will ever admit to, and I'm not proud to say it: I knew all along the Not-So-Good-Guy was indeed a bad guy, so, therefore, I knew I couldn't hurt him or screw him up. I didn't think he had any real feelings, and that made us a perfect pair for a season. I was slowly becoming, or had become, a black hole of yuck, and he already was one. I figured I'd take what I needed from him and let the relationship run its course. That is the most calculated and horrible thing I have ever done to another person.

On the flip side, I also knew that Jason wasn't a black hole. He was good through and through. There was still light in his heart. Jason hadn't turned all dark and sardonic; he loved life and lived to enjoy it. Jason was too good of a man for me to ruin, so I loved him from a distance. Not going after him the moment I knew I wanted him may be the most grown-up thing I've ever accomplished. It took more restraint than anything I have ever done. If I let him in too soon, I would ruin it, perhaps break his heart, and perhaps turn it a little darker than it had been before he knew me.

The two years Jason and I flirted and entertained our crush were fun, but confusing. We tiptoed around our feelings for each other, and whenever my crush hit a peak, his would be at its lowest point and vice versa. I'm sure that poor man never could quite figure out this girl and what exactly it was that she wanted.

Jason has never been a very forward man, so he never tried to force his feelings onto me. He sort of let me do my thing but was never very far away. He dated a couple of girls during those years, and I thought I would die, but I didn't know what the hell I was doing, so I couldn't say a word about it.

Jason's birthday is in December, and every year the guys at 2055 threw a huge keg party to celebrate. I had finally broken things off with Not-So-Good-Guy around Thanksgiving 2003. When Jason's party rolled around in December, I couldn't wait. Maybe I would finally try being honest with him about my feelings that night, and if that didn't work, I would just try to make out with him. If it turned out that he didn't feel the same way about me, then at least I would have had one wonderful night with him. Sometimes, it astounds me how small our brains are.

At any rate, Jason gave me a personal invitation to the party, and I knew that night was going to be my moment. I went shopping for a new outfit and spent more time getting ready than I ever did. I've said that I'm not a very girly girl, but for that evening there was shaving and mascara and probably a curling iron or something, maybe some hair spray. When I got to the party, I immediately began looking for the perfect moment to pull Jason aside and pour out my heart to him. And then, right in the midst of gathering my courage— because you have to get your insides prepared for rejection just in case—*he* showed up. Not-So-Good-Guy walked in the front door, all smiles and jokes. My plan was unraveling before my eyes.

He didn't expect me to be there, so he was just as disrupted by my presence as I was by his. He thought these guys were his friends and he had gotten them in the breakup. So, Not-So-Good-Guy stood on Jason's back stoop, in the rain, pouting. He was the absolute opposite of Jason; he loved being the center of attention. He loved to make a scene and usually did wherever he went. This party was no exception. He tried and tried to get me to go home, and I tried to get him to do the same. When that didn't work, he turned his efforts to trying to get me to go home with him. This night was not going well at all. I don't remember how that situation finally resolved, but I know that by the time it did, it was late into the party and most everyone was wasted, including Jason. The window to profess my undying love had closed.

A couple of days later, I was working at the pizza place when I got a voicemail from Jason. I ran out back to listen to it, and he was inviting me to ride with him to return the keg from his party. He had something to talk to me about, he said. I got so excited I almost fell off the back dock. This was it. Things may have gotten offtrack at his party, but that was OK, because now he was going to say those things to me, instead.

I quickly called him back and said that, of course, I would be happy to ride with him anywhere he wanted to go. We could've been going to a maggot farm or to tour a waste treatment plant, I didn't care. He picked me up at work, and we headed down I-85 South to Frugal McDougal's to drop off the empty shell of his birthday gone by. That's when he said he had a giant crush on our friend Laura. He wanted my advice on what he should do about it.

I seriously considered opening the car door and launching myself onto the interstate, hoping it would be an end to the unbearable misery of that moment. It seemed that all those nights Laura had called him to come to Thomas Street, he was getting the message that *she* wanted him there. All of those nights the three of us were in his bed, he was wishing she were sleeping in the middle, not me. I had waited too long to tell him how I felt, and now it was too late.

Thankfully, Laura was still hot to trot for her ex, another 2055 regular. Jason knew that, and I reaffirmed it. Laura never developed feelings for Jason, so, mercifully, his crush died over time. But not before completely stomping on my heart and making me feel like an enormous fool.

It's a little embarrassing to admit it, but when Jason and I finally did get together, it was my stupid "get too drunk to drive and have to spend the night" plan that did it. My feelings for him never changed, even in light of his for Laura. I knew that was never going to come to fruition, so I chose to be patient and wait it out. By April 2004, his feelings for her had fizzled, and I decided to try again. We got drunk, we laughed, we smoked cigarettes, we listened to music, and then we went to bed. Just the two of us, no Laura. This time Jason wasn't quite the gentleman I had come to know, and, dear heavens, I was thankful for it.

Jason and I have been together ever since that night. I was head-over-heels from that moment on. We began spending most of our time together. Back then, Zach and I split time with Noah fifty-fifty. Noah was with me three nights a week, Zach three nights, and my mother one night. I had four nights each week to spend with Jason, and I did. Laura and I had moved in together, so Jason and I split our time between my apartment and his house. We were having such a good time together, and I finally had something in my life I thought was good. I was still a huge mess, but I felt as if enough time had passed since Zyler's death and Zach's exit that I could have this relationship and not ruin it or Jason.

But Jason was only twenty-five years old. He'd never

been married and didn't have any children, and I had to tell him that I couldn't give him any. I wanted to put off that day forever. I was so afraid it would end our relationship, because he would have to be a moron to stay with me. I came with far too much baggage. For two years, I had been so concerned about breaking his heart or treating him like dirt that I had forgotten the most important part. The cruelest thing of all would be for him to fall in love with me and then discover that I couldn't have kids. For all I knew, Jason was dying to have kids. It may have been the one thing he wanted most in this world, and I had been playing this flirty, "I have a crush on you" game for two years, slowly drawing him in, bringing us closer and closer, just to shatter it all with one sentence and a missing reproductive system. I was an asshole.

I can remember the day I finally told him. I was sitting at the foot of his bed, shaking, and with big tears in my eyes I said that I had to tell him something. He probably thought I was about to admit to cheating on him or that I wanted to break up. Those are the normal revelations that come after, "I have something to tell you." There is no way in the world he could have imagined what was about to come out of my mouth.

I told him about the hysterectomy and how it nearly killed me. For the first time, I told him about Zyler. My sweet Jason sat down next to me, put his arms around me, and cried with me, and for me. No one had ever done that before, not one person. Finally, I felt a little of the darkness in my heart begin to fade. Just a little. Jason and I lay in bed that afternoon and shared stories of the different heartbreaks we had both experienced, and I knew this guy had been so worth waiting for.

Jason has maintained for ten years now that the only reason I'm with him is because he can make me laugh like no one else on this planet. And it's true that he is the funniest damn person you will ever meet. Everyone says so, but that isn't why I'm with him; it's just a giant perk. I'm with Jason because he has shown me what love looks like in a way that no one else has. He believes in me and never once gave up on me when I was a black hole of yuck. In our first year or so together, I broke up with him three times.

Once, we broke up because I wasn't sure he was the guy for me, but I came to my senses pretty quickly on that one. Thankfully, he patiently waited on me to get over myself and took me right back when I asked him. The second time, I was convinced there would come a day when Jason really would want a child of his own, even though he kept assuring me he didn't. He wasn't even thirty years old, yet. How in the world did he know what he would want in the future? Once his friends started getting married and having families, I was certain he would become jealous and bitter because he was stuck with me. He promised that he didn't foresee that day coming, but if it did, he was content with adopting. Eventually, I believed him, so we got back together again.

The third time was the real disaster, and it was a miracle we made it back from that, honestly. I almost killed the most beautiful thing that had ever happened to me. It was around the time when Noah was banging his head into walls at Zach's and bombing out at school.

Zach had come to my house to acknowledge Zyler's birthday. That was something we did for a few years after his death. We would get a cake and some balloons, then Noah, Zach, and I would tell stories about him. We wanted to honor his presence in our lives and not forget the impact he made. We wanted to teach Noah that people still matter after they die. After we put Noah to bed that night, we began to discuss what we could do to help him. Zach suggested the one thing I never in a million years would have imagined.

He asked, "What if you and I got back together?" I was flabbergasted. He said that he still loved me and he always would. He didn't know if we would make a better pair now than we did back then, but he might be willing to find out. I felt my world begin to spin out of control.

I understand now what Zach was thinking and why he said what he said. But you talk about cruel? Of all the rotten things that man had done to me over the years, this may have been the worst. Right then, I was happy and in love. I had finally put him behind me and could conceive of an actual future with someone else.

But I at least had to consider Zach's offer. What if this was the one thing that could make Noah better? What if I did have a chance to put back together the family I so desperately wanted? The dream that Zach had demolished could come true, after all. Maybe, but there were so many what-ifs.

Zach left that night, asking me to promise to just think about it. He hugged me, kissed me on my cheek, and said he loved me. But, even still, I could tell he didn't want me back because he was in love with me. It was mostly for Noah's sake, so I had a lot of thinking to do.

I sat on this information for a week or so, becoming more and more awkward around Jason. He could tell something wasn't right, and I finally couldn't take it anymore and told him the truth. Even if Zach and I didn't get back together, the fact that I was considering it meant I had to break up with him, I said. He didn't deserve that.

With tears and a few strong words, Jason relented and let me go. I know this is hard to believe, but Jason's friends couldn't stand me. I'm sure they thought I was nice enough to be around and enjoyed my company, but they absolutely hated me as a partner for their friend. I had an ex-husband, a kid, no uterus, and I kept breaking up with him. They were right. What in the world did this man see in me, and why was he willing to keep giving me chance after chance? His friends were nice to my face, save one, and he was just plain nasty. But I couldn't really blame them for feeling how they did about me. If this had been happening to one of my girlfriends, it would have been very difficult to keep silent while she threw her life away on some guy who kept giving her the runaround. That's how I would have seen it, at least, but thankfully that wasn't how Jason saw me. For some reason I still don't fully understand, Jason refused to give up on me.

Jason Blackman was my first real lesson in grace. He loved me no matter what, despite my flaws and failures. He saw inside me a heart that could be bright again and determined that he would like to be there when it changed. This is why I'm with him. I hope that doesn't sound selfish, as if I'm with him because he loved me. Sure, that's part of it. His not giving up on me and loving me so deeply is one reason why I want to spend my life with him. But the biggest reason is in all we've been through in ten years, his actions have proven him to be grace-filled, compassionate, and generous. He treated me the way he did, then and now, because that is the content of his character. That is precisely the type of person with whom I want to share my life. I want to be with someone I believe in and for whom I have all the respect in the world. I may have set my sights on Jason first, but he was the first one to love me well and rightly. I can say with all truth that Jason doesn't love me more than I love him. I think we are pretty evenly matched there, but he did teach me how to love him well through how he loved me. In that, he changed me forever. My heart transplant began with him, and I will always be grateful.

So, obviously, I didn't choose Zach. I'm sure he feels that he dodged a bullet there. He didn't really want me, and even though I wanted my family back, I knew it wouldn't be the same. I would have been trading in the only man to truly love me the way a person deserves to be loved. I didn't try to get back together with Jason right away. I think I was too embarrassed and afraid he wouldn't take me back, anyway. I don't know that I would have taken me back.

Several months after we broke up, I let my best friend, Rosa, talk me into attending our ten-year high school reunion. I had no intention of going. The thought of it made me sick to my stomach. All the girls who had gone on to have perfect, little lives and did everything right would be there. I didn't think I could handle facing the reality of that or have it in me to stare down their scrutiny. But Rosa was coming down from New York City, and she assured me that it would be really fun. The booze was free. And she begged, so I gave in.

I've learned in life that most of the time it's a good idea to trust your instincts. That night I did not, and it was hell on earth. No one in the room had had ten years anywhere close to mine. Most of them had graduated college and started their careers and families. One woman had finished college and gone on to be a missionary with her hot missionary husband. She had already traveled the world by the time she arrived at the reunion. The ones who didn't finish college had married their high school sweethearts, stayed in the little town we grew up in, and had kids. They were ridiculously happy trotting their kids off to tee-ball and dance lessons.

Everyone had heard one rumor or another about my life, and they went around the entire night looking at me with pity in their eyes. No one dared asked me about myself and what I was doing with my life. I think they were all too afraid of the answer. A few people did pat me on the shoulder and say, "I heard about your son from my mom. I'm so sorry." I managed to get through it with my friend Jack Daniel's and a few inappropriate jokes. By the time I went to the restroom and was accosted for the fifth or sixth time that night by someone saying they were sorry to hear about my dead baby, I was done in. I marched out of the bathroom and informed Rosa that I was going back to Charlotte and would be at EBs if she wanted to find me later. I took off without a single goodbye to any of my former classmates, my first and last high school reunion in the bag.

I drove straight to EBs, hoping the whole way that Jason would be there. EBs had become like our living room, seeing as we were there most of the nights Noah was with Zach. It was our *Cheers*, and between the time it took us to walk in the door and arrive at our seats at the bar, the bartender had our drinks waiting for us. We never had to ask. So, it was a pretty safe bet that Jason was there.

Being at the reunion and seeing everyone with their spouses, laughing and dancing together, was just painful enough to push me beyond my fear of being rejected or shot down. I had found a man to share my life with, someone I had more fun with than anyone I had ever met. I had found a man who loved me despite all the reasons I gave him not to. I had found someone who made everyone else in the world disappear. When I was with him, we were the only two people in the room, and now I was blowing it. I was letting him slip right out of my life.

I drove as hard and as fast as I could to the bar, ready to do whatever it took to get Jason back. I don't remember what I said or what he said, but I can still see the look in his eyes, the look of hurt and skepticism, as I asked for one more chance. I know I promised not to hurt him again. I probably made lots of promises and said a lot of "I'm sorrys." Some might call Jason a sucker or a glutton for punishment for taking me back, but maybe he was merely trusting his instincts. We haven't broken up since, and that was nine years ago.

On April 19, 2008, Jason and I threw an engagement party for ourselves at Christine's house. We invited about eighty people, I suppose, got a keg and two cases of wine, and Christine made a bunch of delicious food. About an hour after the party started, Jason invited all the guests into the backyard so he could make a toast. Once everyone was settled in, I walked around the corner of the house wearing a wedding dress, and Pastor Jonathan married us right there, in front of the fence blooming with jasmine. Yes, we threw a surprise wedding, and it was the most perfect day of all time.

That morning, we woke up and went straight to Christine's to get ready. Jason mowed her lawn while I got down on my hands and knees and scrubbed her dining room floor. A friend of ours filled the house with beautiful flower arrangements and made me a gorgeous bouquet. Jason's best girlfriends from high school came into town early and served as his honorary groomsmen. They cleaned Christine's front porch and helped put finishing touches around the house.

My mom asked to say a few words during the ceremony because my father had passed away in 2004. He wasn't there to walk me down the aisle, so Dennis did the honors, instead. We wrote our own vows, and Jason prepared some vows to deliver to precious Noah. He promised to take care of Noah and his mom and to love him as well as he knew how. There wasn't a dry eye in the house.

Then our friend Grant came up and sang "The Great Intoxication," by David Byrne. Jason had no idea it was coming, because I had planned that as a surprise for him. I had dyed a blue streak into my hair for my something blue, and we cried as Pastor Jonathan preached the house down using the words of Flannery O'Connor and the Apostle Paul. Did I mention it was the most perfect day?

Later in the evening, Zach came to get Noah, our parents left, and whoever remained drank and partied until 4:00 a.m. Jason and I had our first dance in Christine's living room to our song, "This Must Be The Place" by the Talking Heads. The Talking Heads and David Byrne are kind of our thing.

> "Home—is where I want to be
> But I guess I'm already there
> I come home, she lifted up her wings
> Guess that this must be the place
> I can't tell one from another
> Did I find you, or you find me?
> There was a time before we were born
> If someone asks, this is where I'll be ... where I'll be"

CHAPTER SEVEN
701 CHANCES

One Saturday morning, my friend Laura (a different Laura—it seems most of my friends are either Laura or Lauren) and I were working at the Common Market. Laura is older than me and so much cooler than I am. I didn't actually get to know her until we worked together, but I had seen her around the neighborhood for years. I always thought that wherever she was going was probably where I wanted to be, too. She seemed to hang out with the cool kids, and I imagined their weekends were full of fun and adventures. I didn't know, yet, that Laura used to be Wiccan, or that she had been known for spinning fire at pagan festivals, or that she had just gotten sober. I didn't know that she was doing her best to move away from being one of the sad, cynical people that came through Common Market and into being a person of peace and light.

So, on that particular Saturday morning, as we stood outside smoking our cigarettes, Laura said that she thought she would start going to church. Something was missing from her life, and she couldn't quite put her finger on what it was, and she thought church was as good a place as any to start looking. That was the very last thing I expected to come out of her mouth. I mean, Laura wasn't the church type. When I imagined a sanctuary and all the people inside, we just weren't the kind that fit in.

Still, I had already met with Jonathan by then. I hadn't made up my mind to go to his church, but I figured stranger things could happen than Laura wanting to go to church. After all, I did meet with a pastor after cussing like a sailor in front of him for months.

Laura and I put out our smokes and went back inside, still discussing her church thing. She was saying that she had no idea where she would go or how to even find a good church. She had never done this before.

And then it happened again. There was Jonathan, at that exact moment, picking out gum over in the candy section. How the hell did he keep showing up like that?

I turned to Laura and asked, "You see that guy over there getting gum?" She did. "He's a pastor. He has his own church."

Of course, she didn't believe me at first, thinking I was pulling her leg because of the conversation we were having. I had to promise that I had been to his office not long ago to talk through my crap. I had seen it with my own two eyes. It was real.

Laura marched right over to Jonathan, introduced herself, and said, "So, I hear you're a pastor." He told her all about his church, Renovatus (it's Latin for *renovation*), and when and where it met. And that was the end of that. Laura made up her mind to go the very next Sunday. That was October 2006, and Laura and I are still on this crazy, sometimes scary, sometimes hard, always mysterious and wonderful journey of faith together. That's the story of how it all began for me and for her—two broken, messed up women at The Common Market and a pastor who just kept showing up.

Laura went to Renovatus first, but I followed the next week. We didn't go together the first time because I couldn't get off work. I had a mini-panic attack on my way there. The church met in the auditorium of an elementary school, which

I thought was weird. But at the same time, I was grateful it wasn't some big, old, traditional church building where I would have felt so out of place I'd worry that my presence alone would bring down fire and brimstone from above.

I chain-smoked all the way there, putting out my last cigarette in the parking lot of the school. I'm sure I dressed up because I had no idea what to expect. I can assure you the one thing I most certainly did expect was to be judged. My thoughts about God were iffy at best, and my opinion of Christians was straight up in the toilet. Christians were the most hypocritical, judgmental, conservative assholes out there, and now I was about to willingly walk into a room of them. Hence, the panic attack. How would I be treated once they found out I was a single mother? At this point, Jason and I had moved in together, and, good Lord, what would they say when they found out about that?

I was spiraling out of control and pre-determining all of the outcomes of my foray into Christianity. I had the thing over before it even started. There was no way in hell this little experiment was going to pan out. But, yet, I found myself walking through the door, compelled, borne along you might say, as though I couldn't help myself.

And maybe I couldn't. That's why I say this adventure has been mysterious from the very start. If you find yourself in a relationship with Jesus and at some point along the way the mystery and wonder of it all disappears, you may want to retrace your steps because somewhere you left Jesus behind. Go back and get him.

I knew I had to walk in the door of that church. All of these inexplicable and baffling things kept happening to me. I could ignore them if I wanted. I could. But I was so miserable and heartbroken and in dire need of help. The thing that ultimately got me in the door was that I had decided I wasn't too proud to try anything. So, even though Christians sucked and I was too tough for Jesus, I agreed to put down my pride for two hours one Sunday. I could pick it back up again if I was right about this place.

I never "made a choice for Jesus," and I never said the Sinner's Prayer. I don't have some moment of conversion story to tell. Not long after I came to Renovatus, a new friend, Nathan, gave me a copy of Anne Lamott's *Traveling Mercies*. I absorbed every word of that book. I think I would have eaten it if I thought that would have helped make it a permanent part of me. Reading that book when I did gave me the courage to continue hanging out with Jesus. Anne describes Jesus as a cat that followed her everywhere. She could feel him nipping at her heels, no matter how she tried to outrun him. And try as she did to ignore him, he just wouldn't leave her alone. Finally, after trying and failing to escape him for over a week, she decided, "Fuck it. I quit. You can come in."

That's a lot how I felt about the whole thing. Between Pastor Jonathan just happening to show up in my life and being there when I "prayed" while I stocked the wine, Jason coming along and not giving up on me, and feeling like some of the darkness broke off me when I screamed and cussed at God, I felt like I had no choice but to give ol' J.C. a chance. Fuck it. He was clearly nipping at my heels, and I had a feeling he wasn't going to just walk away.

I may have been willing to give Jesus a chance, but I was unconvinced as to his followers. That first Sunday, I had prepared myself for the worst: hymns out of books, organ music, or terrible worship music like they play on Christian radio stations. Maybe everyone would stare at me, or Pastor Jonathan would preach about condemnation for my sins, and then everyone would have to go around and confess before one another, and then I would just go ahead and die right there on the spot. Maybe they would cast out demons or someone would lay hands on me and try to tell my past and prophesy my future. Clearly, I have a very active imagination when it comes to religious folk.

Worse yet, maybe I would get there and nothing would happen. It would be the most utterly boring morning of my life, and I would leave feeling the same as if I had never been there. Perhaps that is what I feared most of all.

I would be lying if I said I remembered that whole morning in vivid detail. I don't remember the sermon, the music, or where I sat, but what I do remember is important. I was wrong about every single thing, every preconceived notion, every fear. All of them were wrong. When I walked into the auditorium, several people greeted me, smiling as they welcomed me. They said they were glad I was there and meant it. There was coffee, and people were hugging and smiling. The room was full of people who seemed to be like Jonathan and Dennis. The entire space had that same feel to it, like these people had some kind of knowledge I didn't. They were at peace with themselves and the world around them, and I couldn't figure out why.

I love the saying, "We don't know what we don't know." Before that day, I didn't know that the same feeling that radiated off of them could one day radiate inside of me. I didn't know, but I did hope. They possessed something *other*, and I worried that it was something I would never have.

I'm not saying the whole experience was ponies and roses. The music freaked me out. People were raising their hands and closing their eyes in some kind of ethereal trance. I thought it was weird and maybe even silly. Jesus was the object of affection in the songs, and that was completely foreign to me. I wasn't sure how you were supposed to develop affection for Jesus in the first place, so how would I then choose to turn around and sing about it in a room full of people? And, besides, if you have that level of affection for Jesus, one where you are that demonstrative when expressing it, shouldn't you tell him about it in private? That just seemed more appropriate to me.

But then Pastor Jonathan got up to deliver his sermon. While I may not remember what he spoke on, I do remember what it felt like to hear him speak. I sat in the chair in that auditorium crying because, for the first time ever, I felt like someone was telling me the truth. More of my darkness broke off that morning—a much bigger chunk than before.

When Pastor Jonathan spoke of Jesus's character and heart and compassion, I knew that this was the balm all of our souls were so frantically searching for. When he taught me that God is for me and not against me, I thought I would break in half from the endless hope those words unlocked inside me. I had no idea what being a Christian meant. I literally didn't know how to do it, but one Sunday Pastor Jonathan said that when we don't know what to do, all the Lord asks is that we keep showing up.

So, that's what I did. I came to church every single Sunday, and, for the longest time, I was hung over for most of them. I would drink like hell on Saturday night at EBs with Jason and then drag my ass out of bed Sunday morning for church. But I would show up with my notebook and pen, feverishly writing down as many of Pastor Jonathan's words as I could. I couldn't help myself; something kept compelling me.

Pastor never did end up preaching that sermon on condemnation. Instead, he taught me that no matter how many times we blow it, the Lord continues to show up, too. He gives us chance after chance, and even if we've screwed up everything 700 times, God gives us 701. At twenty-nine years old, I was convinced I had the shitty life I had because of all those screw-ups. I figured I had done most of this to myself. I knew I couldn't control Zyler's death, but I had a pretty big hand in all the rest. And now I was learning that the God of the universe would give me all the chances I needed to get it right, that I couldn't ever blow it so badly that he couldn't redeem it. Jesus is in the business of taking things that are ugly or discarded and making them beautiful again. I didn't know what I didn't know.

I fully believed that we live in a world where no one gets what they deserve, good people have truly rotten lives, and bad people have the world at their fingertips. This concept went a long way toward inspiring my disdain for God, but at Renovatus, my paradigm was shifting for the first time. I was coming to truly understand that God doesn't orchestrate our fate; he isn't the puppeteer I had accused him of being. The Lord lets us make our own choices, and then he shows up like a cat, follows us around, and offers to help. And really, no one is all bad or all good, and neither are our lives. We all have a mix of joy and pain. Some of it is our fault, some is our circumstance, and Jesus is there the whole time, waiting to redeem the mess if we'll let him.

That's what Jesus did. He redeemed my messes, all of them. He started by giving me Renovatus as a gift, and it has been one of the most glorious gifts of my life. It took a while, but I finally have that thing radiating inside me that Jonathan and Dennis have. It's peace and joy and contentment. I now know love in a way I never have before, and being loved just for existing and being alive will change every single thing in a person's life. I don't have to perform perfectly or behave perfectly in order to be valuable. I don't even have to have the right feelings in my heart or thoughts in my head. Through the way the people of Renovatus loved me, I learned that all I have to do is breathe, and God loves me.

On Sundays, Pastor Jonathan taught that we are beloved. That was great, but it took the people inviting me into their lives and hearts to know it was true. In the beginning, I wanted so badly to prove these people to be hypocrites, but it turned out that I was disappointed in that. After all my worry, not one person at Renovatus ever looked at me like I had a third eye because I was a single mother. They embraced me and took me in from the storm when I had nowhere else to go. They fed me, clothed me, and said they wouldn't leave me or forsake me. And they never did. I learned that I could trust Jesus because these people proved I could trust them. It took a long time, but eventually the darkness in my heart turned to light. All of it.

I'm not really sure how all that darkness faded away. Looking back now, I can see that I didn't understand what Christianity was about. To me, it was just a set of rules that we are told to live by, and if we do that, we will be pleasing and accepted by God. That wasn't a compelling argument, as

I didn't particularly see what this God guy ever did for us. But over my years at Renovatus, I learned that the things I truly believed and held dear in my heart just so happened to be the same things that were the most true and most dear about God, as well.

Christianity is a subversive religion. It always starts at the margins, a place I am intimately familiar with, and it begins with love. Love is the most important tenet of the faith, and when we are willing to love someone with no agenda and no expectation of receiving something in return, it is a powerful force holding all the potential to change the world one person at a time.

Soon after I came to the church, I was invited on a mission trip to Mexico with Pastor Jonathan; his wife, Amanda; and several other folks. I was the newest Christian in the bunch and knew very little about the Bible or how to minister to people. I was barely able to articulate my faith, but for some reason none of that seemed to exclude me in their opinions. I was invited and included simply because I loved Jesus. They said that made me perfectly qualified.

Not long after we returned from that trip, our church began our small group ministry, led by Nathan. We called them Community Life Groups, and I found myself a part of one that met in Pastor Jonathan's home, led by Amanda. We were a group of oddballs that either worked at night or didn't work at all, so we met on Wednesday mornings. We ate together, prayed together, and discussed the Bible. We also began to love one another and to invest in each other's lives. This is where I learned that it was OK to be vulnerable and to tell the truth about my past and present.

Renovatus takes inspiration from a Shel Silverstein poem that describes who we are: a church for liars, dreamers, and misfits. The church calls itself a church for people under renovation, which includes everyone since we are all in a constant state of renovation. I felt like those things described me pretty well, and if these folks really did mean it, if they really meant that absolutely anyone was welcome, then maybe

I had a chance here. Over time, I came to realize that *all* of the people in my small group were pretty bizarre, indeed. It wasn't just me. And after a while, I recognized that Renovatus truly does let just any ol' weirdo in, and they love them all the same. Including me. I met the best friends of my life in that church and in that small group, and I decided that I had better stay.

Back in those early days, I was still working at The Common Market. Every week, I had to drive across town to Costco to pick up supplies for the store. I stopped by the church office on my way every time.

Tracey was the church secretary. Eventually, she became the executive pastor, but back then we were so small that she was the only person working in the office. I'd come in and ask if she could give me a sermon to listen to on my Costco run. No matter how busy she was, she'd stop what she was doing, select a sermon I hadn't heard yet, make a copy, and give me the CD. It was also free, even though I tried to get her to let me pay something. Many days, I would go back to the office after work and just sit and talk with Tracey for an hour or more. We talked about life and faith, and she taught me about this new religion I found myself so enveloped in. I never mattered what she was in the middle of doing, she always made time for me. I devoured those sermon CDs and my time with Tracey like a woman thirsting to death in the desert. They were ingredients in the elixir that was slowly bringing me to life and will always be some of my most treasured memories.

Renovatus has always been a place brimming with artists. My friend Teddy refers to them as "the Paintbrushes," and it cracks me up every time. Plaza Midwood, the neighborhood where I lived and where the church office was located, began to have Art Crawls once a quarter. Many of the businesses would feature artwork by local artists. Restaurants and bars would have fantastic dinner and drink specials, and the whole neighborhood felt like a giant party. The streets were flooded with people wandering from place to place to support art. So, each quarter our church office would be converted into a wonderful art gallery, complete with food and a DJ. We would sell art made by our congregation members and then donate the money to a local charity that assists people suffering from HIV and AIDS. I absolutely couldn't believe I was attending a Christian church where one of their goals was to offer love and care—without judgment—to the people in our community with HIV/AIDS. This Jesus that Renovatus revealed to me continued to surprise me.

The Lord took care of Noah, too, in ways I never would have imagined. Noah has always been the sweetest, kindest child. He's been easy to raise because his disposition and demeanor are so uncomplicated. But everything else about Noah has been complicated.

He was diagnosed with dyslexia in first grade, thank goodness, because school was a nightmare for him. At some point in elementary school, he was diagnosed with juvenile rheumatoid arthritis, which led to trips to a specialist and all sorts of tests. At the beginning of each school year, I had to warn Noah's teachers that he had lost his brother when he was young and still had a tendency to talk about it openly in class. By fifth grade, my boy was still struggling terribly in school, even though he was receiving therapy for the dyslexia. We ran more tests and found that he had attention deficit disorder. Most challenging of all, Noah couldn't stand his father. They had a very strained relationship, to say the least, and it was hard to get Noah to his father's house without huge amounts of protest.

Then, there were the issues Noah seemed to be suffering as a result of my own depression and general unhealthiness. This was most acute in my years as a single mother. Watching Noah struggle and suffer was heartbreak for me. I lived in a perpetual state of anticipating bad things. Part of my dark heart wasn't just the things that had already happened to me; it was also the knowing in my heart that all the bad things would eventually happen. I lived in a constant state of preparation for when they did, and that's an absolutely miserable way to live. It's hard to get excited or look forward to anything when what you really believe, if you're being honest with yourself, is that anything good or worth having is going to be stripped from you. Brené Brown calls this "foreboding joy", and I had it in spades. But when a person has experienced nothing but one giant loss after another, it's hard to see the world any other way. When Noah was small, I got to the point that none of these complications even surprised me anymore. Each time he was diagnosed with something new or there was a new issue, my automatic response was, "Of course, there is."

Now, I'm no theological scholar (although I would like to be one day), so I don't know how to reconcile all the things that happened after I started a relationship with Jesus. If someone were to ask me to back up my life scripturally, I wouldn't exactly know how. All I know is that when Jesus is involved, there is power and mystery and a truckload of grace. Over the next few years, the grace quotient in my life grew exponentially. I knew how to recognize it because of the grace afforded to me by Jason and then by the people of Renovatus. Mostly, I believe Jesus was able to start turning some things around in my life because, for the first time, I was willing to let him. None of the changes were immediate, but I was finally willing to step onto the long road that slowly led to healing and wholeness. As I allowed myself to be loved and cared for by the people in my new community, as I slowly started to believe I had a new identity in which God called me his *Beloved*, Noah started to even out, too. I took him to church with me and let him be around all that light and love, and I'm pretty sure it wore off on us both. Noah could feel the goodness just as much as I could, and luckily, over time, he began to have a mommy with more good than bad in her insides.

I don't know how or why, but after awhile his arthritis seemed to disappear, too. He's not experienced any pain, and all of his tests have come back clear for years now. And school? The changes there have been nothing short of miraculous. His handwriting is still shit, and going into the twelfth grade now, that doesn't seem likely to change. But he had treatment for the dyslexia and had occupational therapy, and then, when he was in fifth grade, we finally decided to put him on medication for his ADD.

I know none of that sounds like Jesus intervening on my behalf. Those are solutions available to me whether I brought Jesus along for the ride or not. But the teachers, guidance counselors, doctors, nurses, and therapists we've worked with along the way have been kind and diligent. They guided and instructed us without an ounce of judgment or criticism. Not once was I treated like a young mom too dumb to know how to help her son. Every person along the way took Noah's past losses into consideration and loved him as they attempted to help him. Those are the places where I think Jesus met me. Those are the places where he showed me himself and how he cares for me. I believe Jesus always shows up in his people. He is constantly using us to reveal himself because we are the best resource he's got.

I may not be a scholar, but one thing I know to be true and scriptural, is that anything good and beautiful is from the Lord. Throughout the process of Noah getting well, we encountered beautiful person after beautiful person. Today, Noah adores school and makes above average grades. The worst fate that boy could imagine is being homeschooled because he loves going to school so much. That is a remarkable shift from so many years ago. And, even better, Noah adores his dad now. Their relationship has become what I prayed and prayed for over the years. Noah spends one school year with me, and the next with his father. That was his idea, and nothing could be better for my heart.

I spent so many years thinking Zach and I had ruined Noah—that all the hardships Noah encountered in his life were a direct result of Zyler's death and the poor choices Zach and I made in response to it. I had ruined my son. They say one of the stages of grief is guilt, but I never felt overwhelmed by any guilt over Zyler's death. I suppose if I dissected the chain of events leading up to his death enough, I could pull some guilt out, but my gut never told me I was guilty. All of the guilt was reserved for Noah and his life post-Zyler. I've spent more hours than I can count feeling like I failed Noah, and sometimes those feelings still sneak up on me. That's the tricky thing about grief; it comes in all forms and never truly lets you go.

Jason and I dated for four years before we got married. Two weeks before the wedding, grief reared its nasty head and tried to destroy me again. Grief doesn't always manifest in simple sadness or mourning. It can also disguise itself as fear, anger, or depression. This time the fear was out to get me.

The closer the wedding got, the more terrified I became that I was making a huge mistake. I had already ruined one marriage, so why in the world did I believe I could pull this one off? I wasn't so much afraid of Jason and his participation and contributions to the relationship. He had gone out of his way in the last four years to prove his love and devotion. Of course, he wasn't perfect and sometimes, he seriously got on my nerves, but he wouldn't be the one to tank this marriage. I would. Plus, getting married is a huge risk. I was acutely aware of that. It could all blow up in your face. One of us could fall in love with someone else. In five years, he could decide he was wrong and he really did want kids. One of us could get hurt or die.

Sadly, my foreboding joy began to take over. I'm sure it's a protection mechanism, a way of not being caught off guard. I began to think of every single reason why I shouldn't go through with the wedding. I went to Dennis's office one afternoon and sat with him for two hours, meticulously going over every reason why this wedding was a bad idea and I should call it off. Dennis sweetly listened and asked a question here or there, but he never really offered an opinion. He just let me talk it out. I left that day no closer to knowing what I should do.

And then it happened. A couple of days later, I was

driving down Central Avenue, and I did that yelling and crying out to God thing, like I had in my house a couple of years earlier. I told God I didn't understand what the hell he was doing. He had redeemed all the crap in my life. I was now a light person instead of a dark person. My son was doing great. My depression was over. He had redeemed every single thing in my life except for my hurt, loss, and pain over Zach. I was getting ready to get married, but I was still carrying the baggage and hurt of the first marriage. I told God I didn't understand why he would redeem those other things but not this. As I drove and screamed and cried all over my steering wheel, the Lord gently spoke to my heart, "I'm trying to, and you won't let me."

It felt as though a sharp spike had pierced my heart. My tears dried up, and my vision came back into focus. We don't know what we don't know. All along, the Lord had been using Jason to redeem the hurt and brokenness my first marriage had caused, and I just hadn't been aware enough to see it. Through Jason, he was showing me how I deserved to be loved. I was learning how to trust and how to have fun again. This was what it meant to have a life I enjoyed and one that I actually chose. I was learning how to give my heart away again and how to feel safe in that. From that moment on, I never doubted whether to go through with the wedding. Jason and I have been married for seven years now, and they have been the most lovely and redemptive years of my life.

I believe with all of my being that God uses people to heal us. He has other tricks up his sleeve, too, such as scripture, solitude, nature, music, prayer—all things that can lead us into his presence. But the number one way we know he is real and that he cares for us is in the care and compassion of those around us. Between the people of Renovatus and Jason, I can trust that God is good.

Early in my time at Renovatus, Pastor Jonathan preached a sermon series called "The Story of God." He took about four months and preached through the entire Bible in broad strokes, just to give us all a picture of what is in that book and what God is up to. He wanted to show us that if you look at the whole thing, beginning to end, the story really has been going somewhere all along, and it has always been about the people. He showed us how the story is still headed somewhere and how we are all a part of the story now. This is our story. This was my story, and it is headed somewhere. We are his people. This is our history and ancestry, and now we have the chance to participate in the outcome.

That series changed my life. I didn't know that I was a part of a people, that I belonged to a tribe. There is a family and a God that will claim me, fight for me, protect me, and, most of all, love me. Sometimes, I still get pretty emotional from November through the holidays. Zyler was born November 21 and died December 14 of the following year. I don't particularly care for that season most years. It wasn't until I came to Renovatus that I found people willing to let me tell them I was sad on those days and hold my hands while I cried a big, ugly, snotty-face cry all over them. They pray with me, hold me, and tell me how sorry they are that I know what all this feels like. Because of that, I know what it means to have a God that suffers alongside me and whose heart breaks because mine is broken. People, it's the people God sends that change everything. We all are wrapped up in a much larger story that began so long ago, a love story that always has been, and always will be, about redemption for us all.

This sounds like religious mumbo-jumbo, I know. I spent most of my life as a skeptic and critic of anything that smacked of religion. I get it. Also, I don't know how to reconcile what happened to me with the scriptures, except for one instance. In "The Story of God" series, when Pastor Jonathan came to chapter one in the Book of John, he read the passage where two of John the Baptist's disciples meet Jesus for the first time. They are so mesmerized by, and maybe even a little confused by, who this man is that they begin to follow him. He asks what they want, why are they following him? They respond with, "Where are you staying?"

127

How bizarre, right? What an odd response to, "What do you want?" But what they really were asking him is, "Where do you abide?" I think they were so aware of Jesus' otherness, just as I was of Jonathan's and Dennis's, that they were just trying to understand where he and that otherness came from. In what does that otherness abide? Jesus' answer was, "Come and see."

When I said I felt compelled to keep attending Renovatus, that I felt I couldn't help but continue to show up, I think I was responding to John chapter 1. I simply had to come and see. That is my prayer for everyone, every skeptic and every cynic, everyone hurt by this world and our own hard, shitty lives. I hope that everyone will be willing to come and see. I suggest you just give this Jesus guy a chance. He may really surprise you, and it turns out that his people aren't all that bad, either.

CHAPTER EIGHT
BLESSED ARE THOSE WHO MOURN

Jason has been a perfect gift from the Lord. He and Noah get along just fine and always have, but that's the extent of it. They get along fine. I have never felt like the three of us were a family. It has always felt like I had a husband and a son, but not a family. Don't get me wrong; if one were to be divorced and remarried, I simply couldn't ask for a better arrangement. Noah has four parents that love him and care for him instead of two, and the four of us get along remarkably well. I really am thankful. But I started out wanting a family, and, sadly, that dream will never come true.

But then I had a dream on one of the anniversaries of Zyler's death. There was a huge banquet table. The table was overflowing with delicious food and wine, and there were more people around the table than I could even begin to count. There were children and babies and grown-ups, too. In the dream, I was clearly the matriarch of this wild bunch. This was my family. And, most important, there was laughter and happiness ... and more laughter. It was the most incredible, most perfect scene I had ever dreamt. I woke up with my heart feeling more full than it had in a while. The fullness faded to sorrow rather quickly when I realized that it was only a dream and not really my family or my life. Then, just as softly and gently as the Lord can sometimes be, he whispered to me, "Blake, this is your family. When I said I wanted to give you your heart's desires, that didn't mean they would all be realized this side of eternity. But just wait. Your family is coming."

This dream is a comfort and a promise. It's also a reminder of how we all must learn to live in the already/not yet. What does that mean? Is it possible to hold the hurts of this life and still have complete faith in the promises of eternity? I believe so.

Grief Revisited

Last October, my life blew up.

Again.

Without my permission.

Again.

Things at my beloved church fell apart: The church where I fell in love with Jesus and his people, where I went from a dark person to a light person, where I had spent eight years of my life, four of them on staff. I'd had the joy of working side by side with some of my very closest friends in the world, and now, because of the explosion, none of us are on that staff, anymore. None of us attend that church now, either.

Once again, I have found myself in the depths of grief and sadness, searching for meaning in all that has happened and trying once again to reimagine my life and where I should go from here. I am unemployed, and I am without a tribe. This is a place so foreign to me because I have been a part of a people for so long, and still it is utterly familiar because I have spent so much of my life mourning. So, when the ax came down and severed the roots of my tree, I thought, "I've been here before. I know precisely how to navigate this. I'm going to be fine."

The only problem is that I have been far from fine.

Believe it or not, I wouldn't trade the last year and all that I've learned from it. Remember how, during my grief counseling with Dawn, I wished that she had given me a twelve-step program to work through like the people in AA have? I mean, there's an Anonymous for everything: alcoholics, drug addicts, sex addicts, and food addicts. Why hadn't someone thought of one for me? Grief is something just as hard and devastating to overcome, and still no one has come up with a solid program to escort me successfully from one side of the shore to the other.

After all these years, I now know it doesn't work that way. I believe grief is a disease like alcoholism is, and that once you have it, you always have it. Like an alcoholic, you can become a sober griever, but a griever you will remain. I also recognize that I was pretty naïve about how all those addicts live out their sober lives. They never reach some distant shore of sober bliss. They fight each day for the life they have. They have protection plans in place, go to meetings, and avoid their triggers. During my many years as someone who mourns, I had yet to understand this is simply how I must live my life, too.

So, full of cockiness, a survivalist mentality, and an "I'm the one you call in a crisis, 'cause I can handle it" character, I entered this new season. And then I watched as those trademarks of myself crashed and burned, leaving me a charred mass in the rubble. I've been on a new journey of grief this year, one much different than my last. No one is dead, but I'm not sure why we haven't been having funerals. So much has died for many of us, and, unlike my last grief season, I have allowed myself permission to feel these emotions. Sure, I've had some drinks here and there, but I haven't attempted to truly numb anything this time. I have cried more than in all the years of my life put together, I think because I'm not working so hard to repress anything this time around. I have spent time in solitude with Jesus, and I have asked Jason and my mom to hold me when I could no longer function. And so it was during the spring of 2014 that the Lord simply said it was time to write.

In the prologue I mentioned that I felt the Lord nudging

me to write for years but it never felt as if the time was right. I always wanted to tell my story, but that always seemed presumptuous and self-indulgent to me. I could think of no good reason to tell the world about my life. Now, I can think of a couple. First, I believe that we are all in this together. I believe God's story is wrapped up in each of our stories, and he accomplishes his purpose and his goodness through us, so it is right and good for us to share our lives as an encouragement and a testimony.

A friend of mine says that things don't seem real to her until they are said out loud. Well, I say we all say it out loud! Say the hard and awful truths in our lives, so that we all know we aren't alone in our heartaches and disappointments. And then say all the good and beautiful in our lives, so that we can give thanks and share in our joys together. Let's allow our stories to serve as altars to the bitter and the lovely—and the fact that the Lord was present for both.

Second, I think I understand more about grief this time around. The Lord has shown me things I hadn't seen before. In these many months, where it seemed all I had to mourn were the losses I experienced through my church and community, God brought Zyler and my loss of a family back around. He showed me the places in my heart where I still held on to those hurts instead of giving them to him. I had no idea I was still clutching those things with such a tight fist, and I didn't sense how that was affecting me. That being said, I don't want this book to be just a memoir but, perhaps, a type of guidebook. I hope it can serve as a navigation system on your journey of mourning. It's likely that there isn't some program (or boat) we can hop on to safely escort us to the other side, but I believe there are some traveling mercies we can afford ourselves on this never ending road of self-discovery.

Sober Grieving and Faithful Comforting

In a sermon not too long ago, my friend Teddy said that he had been at an NBA game recently. At the top of the game, someone on the PA system spoke about a couple of kids who had died tragically in Charlotte. The announcer asked the crowd to join him in a moment of silence in honor of those children. Teddy remarked on how odd it was that an arena full of people quieted themselves for thirty seconds or so, and then it was over; a basketball game commenced with cheering, shouting, beer, and nachos.

One of the places we get into trouble in America is that this is our idea of mourning. We tend to acknowledge that something has happened, say a prayer, or sit silently for a moment, and then it's over. After that, it's best to pop a pill, get drunk, or go shopping; do whatever it takes to not feel one single bit of it.

In the typical American culture, if someone dies on Wednesday, the funeral is Friday, and everyone is back to work on Monday. That seems odd to me. As I explained earlier, in the Jewish tradition, after the death of a loved one, the family will sit Shiva for seven days. Those days are devoted to visits and meals with friends. There is daily prayer for the deceased and the family left behind. The family doesn't go to work, and in very devout families they may choose not to listen to music or watch television. Often, they cover the mirrors in their homes for up to thirty days. The entire purpose of these rituals is to set aside time for reflection about the deceased person and the part they played in the lives of those still living. I think non-Jewish American culture simply can't handle that level of introspection.

Lately, I've been thinking a lot about the Sermon on the Mount. In it Jesus says, "Blessed are those who mourn, for they will be comforted" (Matthew 5:4). That sounds lovely, and during my first year at Renovatus, I was comforted to hear those words. But I had no idea what they meant. It had been five years since Zyler died and Zach left—and even longer since I lost all that other stuff, like dreams and a uterus—and I still felt lousy.

In Teddy's sermon, he went on to explain that we actually have to mourn. Oh, there it is! That's the kicker. We

133

have to mourn before the comfort comes. That's the part none of us wants to hear, and we definitely don't want to submit ourselves to the process. For five years, I did my best to pretend that all those things really didn't happen to me. If someone asked, I would tell the story with a straight face, not a single tear in my eye. I had convinced myself that this was someone else's story, not mine, so it didn't make me sad when I said it out loud. I would pretend, and then I would self-medicate. So it's no wonder I still felt the weight, the sadness, and the shittiness of it all when I finally landed at Renovatus. No wonder I was dark inside. No one, including me, had ever given me permission to mourn.

Another thing we often overlook or don't make concession for is the multitude of packages grief comes in. There are as many forms of grief as there are human beings. Often, when we imagine grieving, we think only of the death of a person, but that is a gross simplification. We mourn the loss of our dreams or, at least, we should. When things beyond our control happen to us, like my hysterectomy, we grieve. We mourn what might have been and what never will be. We grieve when we wake up at fifty and realize we haven't done the things we set out to do in our lives. We mourn when people let us down and don't turn out to be the people we thought they were. We mourn when *we* don't turn out to be the people we thought we were. We grieve because we see the world for what it really is and see all the injustices around us. We cry out for those we deeply love when they are hurting and broken. We grieve over being flat-out disappointed, whatever form that disappointment takes. We mourn loves that were never realized and never will be. It is OK to mourn any and every loss you have ever experienced, whether it is your fault or not. Give yourself permission. God does, and he will meet you in it and suffer alongside you. I promise.

When I lost Zyler, I was totally alone in my grief. Zach and my mom were too overwhelmed by their own grief to meet me in mine. It was probably all that loneliness that made me a perfect candidate for self-medicating and turning black and bitter. Those aren't good traits for coffee, and they're even worse for humans. I wish we weren't so intimidated by sad people, that we were more comfortable walking with someone who is suffering. I understand why it happens, because I still find it hard to know what to say to someone who has experienced a loss. But people all around us are drowning, and we have the chance to throw them a life jacket.

If you aren't sure what to do, grab some food and a bottle of wine, if you're so inclined, and go to their house. Just go. And as for what to say? You can literally say nothing: Watch a movie, listen to some music, wash their dishes. I can promise that your steadfast presence and willingness to show up will be more than enough. When your friend is ready to say all the awful things in her heart, she will feel safe to do it with you. All we want in mourning is to feel like we are not alone. We want someone in it with us. When the time does come to talk, take a page out of Jason's book. You can cry with your friend because, not only do we not want to be alone, we desperately wish there was someone who would have the courage to mourn with and for us.

Then, you look your friend in the eye and say, "I am so very sorry this has happened to you. I know this feels terrible and that it will for a really long time. I'm here for you. I'm not going anywhere, but I want you to know this won't last forever. You will not hurt like this forever. It may be a long time from now, but it won't be forever."

That's it. It really is that simple. Do you have any idea how many lives could be changed, how many people saved from going over the deep end, just because someone showed up and said words full of hope for their future? If just one person had tried to assure me that the grief I was encountering wasn't my new permanent state, it might not have taken me five years to begin recovering.

And for those who are grieving, please be willing to accept the help. That's what mourning looks like: letting other people in. I took Jason's help, but that felt relatively safe because he was my boyfriend. Others tried, particularly once I became a part of Renovatus. Now, I'm not shy about letting others in and asking for help when I need it. But in the beginning of my time at Renovatus, I tried to keep everyone at arm's length when they legitimately tried to join me in my sorrow.

I know it's scary to be that vulnerable. As long as we live, these will be the most intimate feelings we carry. Grief can be a source of shame, whether you're grieving over something done to you or something dumb you did to yourself. Many times, it makes us feel as though we've failed somehow. For some reason, if it has been years already, it can be difficult to admit you are still suffering as though it were just yesterday. Please, don't feel that way. I have been grieving my losses since 1998, and there are still times I have to let Jason hold me or I have to call a friend and cry. Have the courage to say yes when someone else has the courage to offer to let you cry in his or her lap. It will change the course of your life, and it will change the make up of your heart. And allowing your friend to enter into your suffering with you is good for their heart, too.

I guess that last paragraph begs the question, how long will this last? Forever. I know, I know. You are ready to throw this book out the window and give up because of how uplifting this sounds. Please don't. The things that bring you sorrow stick with you forever. They become a part of your DNA and, try as you might, you can't get rid of them. But you can numb them. Exhibit A: five years of drinking myself into a stupor. Also remember that during that time my heart was becoming more and more dark, and I was becoming more and more a shell of myself. You can choose to go that route, and maybe you need to for a while, but I sure do hope not. The hurt never fully leaves you, but the pain doesn't remain acute forever, either. It becomes a dull ache over time, and then, even further down the road, it will show up so infrequently that it's more like muscle memory pain than actual pain. It's true, I promise.

Finding your way to the other shore

I know I have talked mostly about my experience of church as just the place where I met the people who changed my life, and that is true. However, all those lovely people are not the only reason I continued to show up. I found myself falling deeply in love with the liturgy and the faith of so many that had come before me. I was so disoriented and confused in my own life, and I found that the Church (capital C, not just Renovatus, but the Church that has existed for centuries) served as a North Star for me, guiding me ever toward home.

I didn't go to church because I needed a social club. I went because I found a truth and purity in the practices. I went because it is good for us to believe in something, and then fully participate in that something. I went because there is something about a group of people who share the same beliefs gathering at the same time, in the same place, to participate in their rituals that shapes and forms them into new human beings.

I've talked about coming alive when I think about how this story has been marching on for years and years and now I have a part in it. I get to join the story of my people. Well, I feel the same way about liturgy. The Eucharist and Baptism are examples of practices that have existed long before I ever tossed my hat into this ring. For generations, my ancestors have been participating in those rituals, and they are gifts from God. Pastor Nadia Bolz Weber says that one of the things she loves about liturgy is that it has its own integrity and, therefore, it isn't dependent upon hers. I resonated with that idea. I am a giant mess of a person, and I need something in my life with integrity. I don't lend my virtue to the liturgy, but by joining in, over time, it will naturally begin to reshape mine.

I tell you this because I hope in your grief you will find somewhere that is a North Star to you, somewhere with ritual and character. A place where you don't have to be in charge and the outcomes aren't contingent upon you. I have several friends in AA, and that is one organization chock-full of ritual and liturgy. Its people show up in droves to participate in the same thing, the same way, week after week. I have friends who are obsessed with CrossFit or yoga, which again is the same thing every time. This suggestion has dual implications. A second by-product of participating in something like this is community. Before you know it, you will be meeting friends for coffee or a movie. It will do you more good than I can express to find a group of people who hold beliefs similar to yours and to commit to join in the practices of your particular people. If nothing else, it will keep you up and out of bed long enough to go!

In her book *Bittersweet*, Shauna Niequist talks about having a "home team." Home teams are different than a community. They are the more intimate relationships we develop in our lives. Community is a larger group of people you do life with. My friend Tracey and I like to refer to our home team as the people we would give a kidney to without thinking twice about it. Clearly, that's going to be a much smaller group of people, people who hold a different place in your heart. When I came to Renovatus, I had neither a community nor a home team. And while I have had the privilege of being in community with those people for eight years, it has really only been in the last couple of years that I have developed a true home team. You don't let people on your home team all loosey-goosey, so it can take years to build one. During this new season of grief, I have been so thankful I have people like Jason, Jonathan, another Jonathan, my mom, Tracey, Rosa, Christine, Sheldon, and Common Market Laura. I don't know how I would have survived it, otherwise. These are the people that kept me from looking for help at the bottom of a whiskey bottle this time around.

My suggestions here may seem oversimplified, but in my early years of grief, I honestly didn't have a soul to tell me that I would drown without a community to hold me up and a home team willing to do the heavy lifting for me. So, I'm telling you. If you don't have these people or these structures

in place in your life, get them quick. Join a church or a gym or
go back to school. Make some friends that count, and after
that, make some friends to whom you'd be willing to give
your kidney. Those people will be the difference between
giving up and being willing to face another day.

Also, I hope very much that you will allow some room in
your life for the mysterious and the supernatural. You don't
have to be a part of a faith community to recognize the
unexplainable in your life. All I'm asking is that you notice
things like what happened when I was stocking the wine, was
in dire need of help, and Jonathan "just happened" to be
there. Since that day, the mystery and wonder of the world
and the God who created it have been all around me. There
are the examples from your own life. In mine they are Noah's
arthritis disappearing or when I sensed the voice of the Lord
when I was so unsure of marrying Jason. I have a thousand of
those stories from the last eight years, and so do you if you
pay attention. But what's interesting to me is that I have a
thousand more from the eight years prior, I just didn't know
how to see them, yet. When I began noticing those little
things that we sometimes refer to as *coincidences*, it went a long
way toward helping me feel as if I wasn't alone. Those little
moments made me feel seen and known by God, and they are
still happening today.

After I left my job at Renovatus, I went to work briefly
at a health food store. On my first day, I was terribly nervous.
What if I didn't fit in? What if I didn't make any friends? Plus,
I was grieving getting into my car to go to work when that
work was not for Renovatus. See? Grief really does come in
all sorts of forms, and many will take you by surprise. As I
got ready that morning, I was just a wreck, so I prayed, asking
the Lord to show me grace on that first day, to give me
something to show that he was with me and that I would be
OK. I cried a little, and I felt like throwing up a little, but off
to work I went.

As soon I got there, I went into the break room for a
moment. The first guy I met was someone who had been

attending Renovatus on and off for years. He said that he had been there several months before on a Sunday when I had preached. Then we talked about how much we both loved the church and Pastor Jonathan. I could not believe it—he was the very first guy I met and already I felt much more at ease and at home in this new place. Then, I went downstairs to start my shift. As I was getting water from the cooler, I saw that one of the customers sitting nearby was also a friend from Renovatus. We chatted, and he gave me a hug, and I felt so much more relaxed. It felt like the Lord had heard my cry of fear and anxiousness, so he sent me a little boost to say, "You're OK. I'm with you."

When I first became a Christian, I had all the same big theological questions as the next guy: Can you explain heaven and hell? What do you mean by "the Father, the Son, and the Holy Spirit"? What do angels do? And on and on.

But people often want to talk about miracles, and many contend that those were merely stories that happened during the time of Jesus, not something we see today. I strongly beg to differ. To me, all of these perfect, little oddities that happen in my life—that I can't seem to find an explanation for—are my miracles. I don't need to see writing in the sky or a bird landing on my shoulder and audibly speaking the promises of God. Waiting for signs and wonders that bold is ludicrous. What small things happen all the time in your life that make you wonder or bring you delight? Don't rush past these things. Give them your attention. Take a moment to feel gratitude in your heart for them. Those little moments when you feel known by something bigger than yourself—those are your miracles. They belong to you only, and they are a treasure. They are mysterious and supernatural, and opening your heart to them will allow some of the pain and cynicism of this sometimes-cruel world to peel off.

That's it. That's as profound as it gets for me. Your guide to navigating grief is that simple; at least it's that simple to state. It is infinitely complex in practice. If you will remember these tips—ritual, community, home team, and recognizing the mysterious—you will find life again. I have tons of friends who are grieving the loss of something right now, and I always tell them the same thing: "You *will* love your life again." And I say that to you, too, dear friend: You *will* love your life again!

It's also true that some of these hurts simply won't be fully healed on this side of the Kingdom of God. We'll have to hold some of the hurts gently until the day that all of our dreams come true and we are reunited with everyone who has gone before us. That is by far the hardest part of grief and loss. The hardest. There are days for me when the only thing that is able to reconcile that fact even slightly is John 16:33: "I have told you these things, so that in me you may have peace. In this world you will have trouble. But take heart! I have overcome the world" (NIV).

Long before I worshipped Jesus, I worshipped at the altar of the Indigo Girls. I still do, a little. Outside of the Lord, there are three people who have shaped and formed my life the most, Pastor Jonathan and the Indigo Girls. Starting way back when I was a girl, they sang the song, "The Language or the Kiss," that became a sort of hymn for me. I would listen to it over and over, watching the path my life was taking and praying that this song wasn't my self-fulfilling prophecy. The day after the dream about the banquet table and my family, I got up and played that tune once again. Toward the end of the song, sweet Emily Saliers sings: "Oh mercy what I won't give/ To have the things that mean the most/ Not to mean the things I miss." Looking back now, thankfully, I can say I don't think that prophecy has come true. And looking forward, I can also say I don't think it ever will.

EPILOGUE

A month or so ago my friend Tracey invited me to attend a Breathwork class with her at a little yoga studio. The class description on their website reads like this:

"Breathwork is a perfect healing tool for the twenty-first century. One session alone can change your life; its effects are immediate and permanent. Breathwork is a powerful and effective way to heal past traumas, offering an alternative and healthy way to release old pain, grief, anger, or other unexpressed emotions. Breathwork brings about changes in a person's relationships to themselves, others and the world in their overall mood and life perspective, and in their sense of connectedness."

It seemed like a great idea for us during this season of grief and mourning. She was certainly hoping for a healing breakthrough, and I was just happy to go along for moral support. Off we went with the supplies we were asked to bring: our yoga mats, pillows, blankets, and eye masks.

Once we were in the room, the instructor gave a fifteen-minute or so explanation of what we would be doing and what we could expect to happen. It was mostly a longer version of what is on the website thrown in with some of the instructor's own personal experience. None of this sounded scandalous to me. It was maybe a little odd but not scandalous.

I am a firm believer in the mystical. I believe it's possible to transcend this time and space and have supernatural, mystical encounters with the Lord. So when the instructor said we might see visions or have out of body experiences during the class, I quickly decided it was time to put my money where my mouth was. I either believe in that kind of thing or I don't. As the music began and I lay down on my mat, I decided that I did believe and that I would have an open mind.

During the next hour, I proceeded to have the most spiritually intense (and what felt traumatic at the time) experience of my life. We all began breathing in deeply and loudly through our mouths. Then we let our exhale fall rather silently. This continued for what could have been five minutes or an hour. I wasn't sure. The music is so loud during the class that you can barely hear anyone else in the room. Their breathing is drowned out and so is most of their sobbing or wailing. Yes, some people sobbed and wailed—including me.

When the instructor explained the process, I thought it entirely possible that I might have some healing experience from all that had been happening at the church, maybe some leftover feelings about Zach, or even from my relationship with my mom when I was a teenager. Never in a million years did I suspect that I still carried deep hurts left from Zyler. I mean, I have spent the last thirteen years healing from that. That's done, and while I still get sad during the holidays or on his birthday, there isn't any new information to discover. There aren't any hurts there that I am unaware of. I know them all by now.

So, when I closed my eyes, began to breathe, let the music drown out my fellow breakthrough seekers, and began to see images of my sweet little baby, I almost lost it. Well, I did lose it, eventually. I saw images of a pea pod, and it was clear that one of the peas was Zyler. I could also feel the presence of the Lord so thickly and tangibly, not only in my spirit's and mind's eye, but also physically hovering over me in that room. I could feel that the Lord had his arms wrapped around the pea pod and that this clearly represented Zyler before his birth. The Lord had him before he was born with a broken body.

The next scene I saw was Zyler as a toddler, running and playing. Of course, as humans we only have human references, so the place where he was looked an awful lot like Rivendell from *The Lord of the Rings*, which is to say, it was gorgeous. It was obvious that he was there with God. Then I saw Zyler again, as a seven- or eight-year-old child in the same place, also with God. The Lord was all around, in the trees and the grass and in the very air Zyler was breathing. It was impossible to separate the two of them. It was hard to know where Zyler ended and God began ... or where creation ended and God began. It seemed they were all beautifully and perfectly woven together. Zyler was alive, and he and all of creation breathed with the very life of God running through their existence.

Then the Lord showed me Noah. He was a man, and he was not where Zyler was. It was as though the Lord himself was pushing Noah toward me here on the Earth. Noah was bright and shining, and I don't know if that was supposed to represent him being an angel or if the light coming from behind him was God sending him to me. Either way, the message was clear. The Lord said to me: "I have Zyler. He is here with me, alive and safe. Now is the time for him to be with me and for Noah to be with you. He is your gift, and this is your time with him." During this moment *Amazing Grace* came on, but it was being sung in some other language, maybe Latin. Then it changed to *Ave Maria*, and I thought I would split absolutely in half. I lay on the floor of the studio and wept like I hadn't in a very long time.

After that, the instructors came around, rubbed each of our heads gently, and said it was time to switch back to our normal breathing. That was when all hell broke loose for me.

Our instructor had warned us that often when we switch to the normal breathing, we have the most profound experience. I didn't think I could take anything much more profound than what had just happened to me, but, again, I was trying to stay open.

There are two important little tidbits to note here. First, anytime I'm somewhere like a yoga class where I have to lay with my hands by my sides, I always place my hands on my lower belly, instead. Second, after Zyler died, I wasn't suicidal, but I honestly believed that Zyler had not simply ceased to exist. He did exist somewhere. I would lie in bed, sometimes for hours, trying to figure out a way to get to wherever he was. I just wanted to be there, not here. I guess subconsciously I knew the only way I could get to him would be to die myself, but I don't recall ever lying there wishing I was dead. I just wanted to find him and be with him.

As we changed over to normal breathing in the class, I placed my hands on my lower belly and assumed I simply was going to relax after all I had just seen and experienced. Instead, a feeling started to rise inside me, and I knew from the bottom of my little toes that what I was feeling was the truth, a new truth that I had not recognized before. It was a truth I had carried with me for years but had never acknowledged.

Since the day Zyler died, I had maintained that I didn't feel guilty about it; I never thought it was my fault that Zyler didn't live. But that night, I knew it wasn't true at all. All of a sudden, the words, "I killed my baby. My body killed my baby," began to ring in my ears, and I understood what I have believed all along but never would admit. One more awakening experience waited for me: All these years, I have wished I were dead. I have never stopped wishing I could get to Zyler. I wanted to be where he is, not here. This is why I have always felt like there was a distance between Noah and me. This is why I have trouble fully entering into joy and gratitude.

I frequently and secretly judge folks who can't seem to

function after the loss of a loved one, especially if they have children that need their care. Of course, I compare them to myself: *I continued to get out of bed, so why can't you? I took my ass to work, so why can't you?* Right then, I realized I was far more similar to them than I cared to admit. I may be in an upright position, holding a job and paying the bills, but in some ways I am still an emotional train wreck with many still-unresolved issues. This time I didn't weep. I sobbed and wailed so much that the instructor came over, rubbed my head, and whispered into my ear that I was going to be OK. Everything was going to be OK.

After our session had concluded, we went around the room and each person gave a one-word descriptor of how the experience made us feel. My co-breathers said, "Beautiful," "Humble," "Grateful," and so on. When it was my turn, I told the class that I was traumatized. Some of them looked a little shocked and taken by surprise. I didn't mean to be the odd man out, but I never in a million years suspected that I had unfinished Zyler business and that I was angry. I wanted to keep my heart in the safe cocoon I had built for it since I had begun a relationship with Jesus. I was convinced I had done all the hard work of grieving that loss and that being with Jesus was enough to handle it. It turns out that simply wasn't true.

Thankfully, I spent some time with Pastor Jonathan later in the week and told him the whole story. By the time I got to him, I was still angry. What was the point in knowing that I really hold myself and my faulty body responsible? If my body were tip-top, I wouldn't have needed a hysterectomy and my womb would have grown a baby with no holes in his heart. How is it helpful to know that I have been—and I suppose continue to be—wishing I were with Zyler all this time?

Pastor Jonathan didn't have any clear-cut answers to my questions, but he did talk to me about our true selves and what it means to know that part of us. We talked about integration of head and heart and knowing the depths of what all is in us. During the Breathwork class, I got upset with the Lord after he showed me where Zyler is and that Noah was for me. I'm often getting upset with the Lord, and, mercifully, he never responds to that feistiness with anger, only kindness. I was upset because I didn't understand why the Lord does things the way he does. Why is Zyler there and Noah here? Why can't we all be together? Why do we live in a world where we experience so much loss and pain? During that period of frustration, I felt God hovering directly over my face saying, "You already know all the answers. You already have all the answers. You know, you know." I knew he was right.

Pastor Jonathan and I talked about God planting the truth and himself deep in our cores. We know the truth because God is truth and he lives inside us. Getting intimately familiar with our true self is always the best thing for us. I believe it makes the space between the Lord and us smaller and smaller. Jonathan also reminded me of why he believes the Lord appeared first to Mary Magdalene on the day of his resurrection. He said it was because she needed it the most. That made me cry. I have lost more than most, he said, and because of that, the Lord has also comforted me more than most.

While I was still pretty frustrated with the idea that the Lord brought me any comfort whatsoever in that class, Jonathan reminded me that the Lord took me to where Zyler actually is. Right now. Today. I have seen him, and I know that he is alive and happy and safe and with God. How much more comfort could I receive? It seems that in my anger, I overlooked the most beautiful gift I have received since the dream of the family banquet. Thank God, I have a home team to point out my blessings when I can't see them for myself.

That very night I began to get sick. That was close to five weeks ago now, and I'm still not fully well. I have been to four different doctors and taken a million medications. Maybe I exaggerate, but it's been a lot. I give myself breathing treatments and squirt shit up my nose, something I swore I would never do. I stayed with my mother for a week because Jason is working out of town this summer and I was pitiful and needed someone to take care of me. I cough and blow my nose all day and generally feel sorry for myself. During this time, Noah went off to camp, and I absolutely couldn't wait for him to get home. I've missed Jason while he's been away more than I could have imagined and gained a deeper understanding that I am just not OK without him, even when I'm completely well physically.

About a week or so ago, I was in the shower. I talk to God in the shower. It's kind of our thing. This day I was feeling particularly weepy. I missed my church and my old job there. I missed Jason and was so tired of being sick. I was just grieving all the things. In the middle of my tears, the Lord spoke to me. I haven't been this sick in a very long time. Jason and I have been together for ten years, and he says he has never seen me this sick. The Lord reminded me of how hard I have worked to get well. I have fought to kick this and gone through every channel I knew how to find an answer. He drew my attention to how much I couldn't wait for Noah to return from camp and how desperate I am to get to my husband because he makes me feel like a whole human being. And safe. And happy. He makes me feel all that. Then the Lord, in that sweet way that he has, said that to him, those all seemed like things a person who wants to live would do or feel. He said that deep down I actually *want* to live. I felt my insides burst with relief and joy.

Grief doesn't stop. It doesn't totally wreck you or kill you, either. If you allow the Lord to do the things only he can do, grief will leave you better off than it found you. It has taken me going through this current round of grief, when my life blew up again, to believe that. But I sincerely do.

I would like to leave you with this. As I was looking through some old writings for this book, I found a story I wrote in 2008. It isn't that good, and it can be downright cheesy in places. Also, I don't love my writing style from back

149

then, but I'm including it here, anyway, unedited. I said in Chapter 3 that I didn't want Noah when I got pregnant with him. I thought that having him would ruin my life. As it turns out, he is the very first gift the Lord sent to save me. The Lord redeems every single thing—all of the sadness, all of the mistakes, all of the heartbreak, all of our shit. He will make something beautiful out of our mess, if we'll let him. I'll let this story serve as my altar to all that God has redeemed for me through Noah.

~

It's the night before Zyler's eighth birthday. So much has changed, while so many things are the same. I am still broke as hell, wondering day-to-day how to stretch the little bit we have. The money thing I am used to. I don't think I would know what to do if I had money. But what surprises me year after year is the way I feel on this day and really the rest of the holiday season. Around this time, a sadness kind of lands on top of me like a blanket on a cold night. And just like that, I seem to snuggle right in down and deep whether I mean to or not. Each year, you know, sometime around summer, I think, *This is the year I have it licked.* I feel so good, and I pat myself on the back for making progress, and all seems right with the world. I mean, come on, this year I was able to start my own support group for those struggling from the horrible, insane emotions that come with the death of a loved one. Now, that is progress! I just knew for sure this November and December would come and go like nothing ever happened. But here I am—the night before his eighth birthday—crying like a little girl.

After Zyler died, I thought it was pretty shitty that God had left me with Noah to take care of. Then, after Zach left, I was really pissed at God for leaving me all alone in this world with a four-year-old to look after. All I wanted to do was nothing. Nothing seemed like a real good option to me at that time. And by nothing I mean self-medicating with plenty of alcohol, hanging around tons of rotten people, and smoking enough cigarettes to kill a small village. Being a provider, comforter, caregiver, and role model for Noah was really getting in the way of that. Now don't get me wrong, although I made mistakes, Noah never once saw me drunk or out of control. He may have seen me act like an ass once or twice or been around on days I had a hard time getting out of bed, but God gave me enough grace to pull myself up by my boot straps every day and do what needed to be done.

Now, it's seven years later; I am not drunk, and I don't smoke nearly as many cigarettes, anymore. I still hang around rotten people, but that's mostly cause I believe we are all rotten to an extent. I don't smoke much, and I rarely drink just simply because I don't want to. Trust me, that doesn't surprise anyone more than me! But I have to say, on a night like tonight, it is taking everything inside of me not to go sit in a dark bar, burying my feelings with delicious, warm whiskey. Then, once the feelings are good and safe somewhere really far away, I could put an extra deadbolt lock on them with about eight hundred cigarettes, and about this time is when I would really shine. I would feel so good at this point, I would just be sure that another whiskey and a terribly deep conversation about Jesus, death, and the nature of the human race would be a really good idea. I would feel smart and numb and sad and alone and really happy I wasn't sober. It could be a great night!

But I had to go and "find" Jesus. The real Jesus, not the one I love to drone on and on about when I've had a few drinks. My amazing pastor, Jonathan, teaches us to pray that God will change our want to. See, in the last seven years there have been many, many nights like the one I just described, so many that it seemed going to the bar was just a normal reaction to an emotional dilemma. Over time, I have grown to hate this "normal reaction." It's expensive financially and physically as it costs your health after awhile. And it's the same people night after night, just drinking their lives away. It breaks my heart to see the brokenness in their faces because let me tell you—the only people at a bar night after night are folks who have forfeited their hearts and souls for the Almighty Emotion Killer.

It's been about two years now since God and I got back together. I study him, and he loves on me. I talk to him, and he talks back. I cry sometimes, and he puts his arms around me. Without knowing what I was doing, I prayed that prayer. God, please change my want to's! I always felt a little ashamed cause I could just imagine other Christians praying that same prayer. I figured they had things in mind like gluttony, materialism, and judging others, and here I was hoping God would deliver me from WANTING to go drink and smoke my sadness away at a bar. (Or a friend's house. I'm not picky).

There are some things I have learned over the past couple of years. I have learned that I love Jesus more than I love Jack Daniel's. I have learned that for a while bars, booze, and cigarettes were my gods. I also learned a little bit about this idea of letting yourself die so that Jesus can come live in you, instead. That is the scariest part of being a Christian for me. Why do I have to die so that Jesus can be a part of me? Well, here is what I know: When I was the most full of me, I was the saddest, most cynical, most bitter person I knew. I made horrible choices and saw the world through a lens of total disgust. But once I began to pray that God would help me stop serving myself, little by little my heart started to breathe clean air again. You know what I figured out? When I let Jesus in instead of the other gods, he never, ever chooses things for me that will turn my soul black. All of Jesus' choices are white and clean and they smell good. They are light, and my choices were all heavy and sad. His are happy and naïve and sweet and tender. And now I am happy and naïve and sweet and tender for the first time since I was a teenager. Some may disagree, but I think that is a good thing.

Another thing I have discovered in these last two years is that God is much more wise than I am. I know, I know. I should've known that all along, but I am stubborn and I was mad. I was also suffering the many, many delusions that come with extreme grief. It has been a long, arduous journey, one racked with self-loathing, self-denial, confusion, and, oh, so much pain. But guess what? God knew what he was doing when he let me keep Noah. Or maybe he let Noah keep me. Noah is the only reason I got up and kept going. In the middle of all my cynicism and black outlook on life, there was maybe a part of me that thought we could be redeemed. I would look into the face of my one remaining perfect child, and there was hope in his eye. He had happiness and innocence and joy, and I thought maybe, just maybe, there is something good left in this world. What if I had had my way? I would have let Noah go, too. I would have been without hope for sure. I would have gone long and hard after a path of self-destruction because I would have had nothing to hold me back from it.

I didn't decide to walk through this life with the Lord for Noah. I decided it because of him. Sure, I knew my despair and darkness were ultimately hurting Noah, but I didn't get better *for* him. It was because Noah showed me that we can stand on the edge of hell about to fall in, and somebody just might be willing to pull you back again. The Bible says that unless you have the innocence of a child, you cannot enter the Kingdom of Heaven. It was Noah's innocence that taught me there is still goodness and beauty in the world. Through his innocence I learned to stop serving my own selfish ugliness and serve something more whole, healthy, and pure. His innocence led me to the Kingdom and gave me back my innocence. Can you imagine where I was? My youngest son is dead, and my husband has left me … but God was wise and merciful. He left me a four-year-old to guide me and love me! We humans couldn't think of things that incredible if we had a lifetime to try.

It's one in the morning now. I have one more hour left to hit up some bar. I could put some money in the jukebox and dance the same dance I have danced on this night for the last several years. I could be witty and philosophical. I could be zoned out and feeling nothing. But I think I finally came to a fork in the road. Maybe the fork has always been there and I have just been too wrapped up in me to acknowledge that I had another choice. I think this will be the year I exercise my right to choose. I'm gonna go hang out with Jesus, instead.

ACKNOWLEDGMENTS

It would be silly of me to write a book about all I've been through and not express my forever gratitude to the people who have loved me well and kept me safe along the way.

Rosa Karim and I have been together since we were five years old. That's a long, damn time. We may live roughly six hundred miles apart, but she has never been far from my heart. Rosa, thank you for never letting the physical distance equal an emotional one. And thank you for being the only person who has always honored my role as a mother with a Mother's Day card year after year. Those cards have meant more than you will ever know.

How could I have survived even a day without Christine Pratt? Christine, you have been my sister and my constant. It's been eighteen years, and you've never left me. I mean, let's be honest, I never left your crazy self, either. We've both been handfuls over the years, haven't we? You've fed me, housed me, listened to me, and loved me. You're also never short on cigarettes and wine, either! I will always be thankful I get to spend my life dancing to the *Practical Magic* soundtrack with you!

TRACEY!! Who gets to make a lifelong best friend when they are little, then another when they're in their early twenties, and yet another as a grown woman? Thankfully, the answer is me. Tracey Rouse, you have changed my life. You teach me everything, you believe in me, and care for me in ways I didn't know I needed. You make me believe I can do most anything. Thank you for letting me be your person. I love you, Kidney!

Jonathan Simmons, Laura Henson, and Sheldon Lynn are my home team. Years of memories, hours upon hours of conversation, and more laughs than I can count. You guys never let me fall flat on my ass without being there to pick me back up. Jonathan, I can't wait for the day I get to be your groomsman. Or the day I'm the proud father at Gabe's graduation, Laura. And Sheldon, I'm counting the days until we ride through the country drinking Cheerwine with the windows down singing *Boogie Shoes*!

Jonathan Martin made me want to keep saying yes to Jesus. Every time I was full of doubt or so afraid I just wanted to run, you were there. The way you see the world helps me make sense of it. The Gospel you believe and call Good News always sounds like life to me. I tell people God used you to bring me back from the dead. Thank you for all you've done for me. Thank you for calling me friend and always being willing to claim me. I couldn't be more grateful the Lord put you and me together.

My mother, Tootie Broome, has become one of my closest and dearest friends. We had a rocky start, didn't we, Mom? I know you always joke that I'll say the worst when it's time to talk about you. But I only want to tell everyone who has a tough relationship with a parent to be patient and to be kind. They could be in for the most rewarding relationship of their lives. I love you more fiercely and more deeply than I ever would have thought possible. I'm so glad I got to be

ACKNOWLEDGMENTS

your kid. Also, I'm taking this opportunity to publicly state that whatever the topic—I'm right!!

My husband, Jason Blackman, is always and forever my favorite. Whatever crazy thing I have wanted to do, from fundraising my salary when I went to work at the church to pushing you not to work a regular 9 to 5 so you could pursue acting and film production, you've gone along for the wild ride. There's so much I want to do in this life, and you never tell me no. You encourage me and help make a way for me. I wouldn't be me without you, baby. I love you with my whole heart.

Last, this book absolutely would not exist without my amazing editor and publishers, Tim and Kristen Driscoll. I remember the first time Kristen heard my story and told me I needed to turn it into a book. She told me she would help make it a reality, and she meant it. She and Tim have believed in this project from Day One in a way I have never experienced. I have more confidence that I can accomplish the things that matter to me because they took a chance on me. Thank you both from the bottom of my soul.

Made in the USA
Lexington, KY
07 August 2015